# Prepared

*Discovering what God has prepared for you*

An in-depth study of Ephesians 2:10

ISBN: 978-0-89098-914-2


2809 12th Ave S, Nashville, TN 37204


Cover design by Jonathan Edelhuber and Debbra Stephens

*All praise to the God who prepared me*
*throughout this study—*
*the masterful God who prepares me still.*

## *Dedication*

For Mark and Rob, devoted brothers without equal and loved beyond measure; and their lovely wives, Carol and Yvonne, my dear sisters-of-the-soul.


## *With Special Thanks*

To Mark and Carol for showing such love and compassion and for faithfully being God's instrument of blessing.

To my Burnt Hickory family for their unceasing prayers and encouragement.

To Virginia Day for showering my family with purest love. Your devotion as a servant never ceases to amaze me.

To 21st Century Christian Publishing for partnering with God in His masterpiece-creating business that nourishes the faith of women.

To the fine folks at 21st Century Christian, especially Tom Tignor and Stacey Owens, for using their expertise and talents on the polished finish.

And with sincere appreciation for the readers for endeavoring to be more prepared through the study of God's Word.

# The story behind the study

Some mornings I find myself more teachable than others.

In the quiet of one such morning, I arbitrarily opened my Bible to the second chapter of Ephesians. My eyes landed on an already highlighted verse—Ephesians 2:10: "For we are God's workmanship, created in Christ Jesus for good works, which God prepared beforehand, that we should walk in them" (ESV).

I read the familiar verse slowly; feeling encouraged by the confidence packed in those words of purpose. Suddenly, I was struck by one word in that verse: *prepared.*

The life of the man who penned that verse quickly animated my thoughts. I was intrigued by all the ways God had prepared Paul and how his life epitomized the profound statement he made.

I camped there for days.

With each thing Paul experienced, God prepared him for the next. And that next thing prepared him further for what God had for him next. And on it went.

God prepared him...to do the work He had prepared *for* him.

*Prepared*...in that moment I liked how that word fit. And I nodded my head, as if in agreement, that the season from which I was emerging was definitely a period of preparation and that in all our seasons, God prepares us for what He has *for* us.

If only I could tell you how many times in the past ten years I've written about waiting.

Waiting on the Lord.

Waiting in the Lord.

Waiting before the Lord.

But do you know what I have finally learned, *at last?*

That in my waiting God was preparing me.

Now, I didn't realize at the time that's what He was doing, mind you. (*You know what they say about hind-sight!*)

I would like to sound all clever here and tell you that I knew all along God was preparing me; and exactly what He was preparing me for. Though He has brought me to this new and unfamiliar season in my life, and though I know not what lies ahead, I do know He has been preparing me for whatever that may be. (I also know that He will faithfully provide what's lacking.)

When my children entered high school, my mother's prayer became common to most. Don't we all, at some point in time, utter; "What's next, Lord? After the kids are grown and gone...what do You have next for me?"

There *is* an answer to that prayer.

In contemplating Ephesians 2:10 that one morning, I looked back. And when I did, it was as if God parted a foggy veil that shrouded that waiting season. I was finally able to see one important thing: God had been preparing me for the what-next. Because He does, in fact, have something prepared *for* me.

As He does for you!

Whatever your circumstances may be, know that God is preparing you for that next thing, too. Right from where you are, in fact.

Am I prepar**<u>ed</u>**? Past tense?

**NO!**

But, I am **MORE** prepared...and being prepared still. That is my most earnest prayer—that He will indeed continue the work He started. And do you know what is even more glorious? It pleases Him to do so! For all of us.

Together, shall we willingly place ourselves before our Maker for the preparing?

We **can** trust that in His perfect wisdom and perfect timing He will provide for our understanding what He has prepared *us* for. And what He has prepared *for* us.

Because He is—ever and always—a God who prepares.

# TABLE OF CONTENTS

*WEEK ONE*

# The Essence of Prepared

**DAY 1**

## Introducing Preparedness

A new day dawns and—no matter what waits to greet you—there is nothing quite like feeling **prepared**.

What was waiting for you at the start of this new day? Was it the familiar and expected? Or was it something more challenging?

And how did you rise to greet it? Were you reluctant? Apprehensive? Indifferent? Or did you feel prepared?

How prepared *can* we be?

And just what is "it" that prepares us?

Together, we'll be exploring more fully what the "it" is that prepares us. And then, we'll follow that trail to see where it leads us in discovering what it is we're prepared **for**.

But first, let's see what our Lord has to say on the matter…

Prepared—adj.: "Properly expectant, organized, equipped; ready."

Prepare—verb: "To put in proper condition or readiness; to make ready in advance for a particular purpose or use."

(*Dictionary.com, n.d.*)

## Feasting Preparations

Don't you love preparing for special feasts? Whether it's a significant occasion, holiday or church potluck? But isn't it really more about being with those gathered around the table than the meal itself?

One of the parables Jesus directed to the religious leaders of His day, during the final week of His earthly ministry, is about a feast God is preparing for His people. And it gives us a glimpse into that for which we should ultimately be preparing.

**Read Matthew 22:1-15.**

According to verse 2, what is the Kingdom of Heaven compared to?

A wedding feast

The feast is prepared for His son Christ.

Which is Whom?

The feast is given by the father.

Which is Whom? God

"Blessed is the one who will eat at the feast in the kingdom of God."

(*Luke 14:15*, *see also Rev 19:9*)

Who is entrusted with the inviting (vs 3)?

Servents

From verse 4, circle what it is that's "ready":

Nothing

Only some things

Everything

Two groups ignored the invitation (vs 5), what did "the rest" do (vs 6)?

siezed slaves & kill them

Was the feast prepared anyway (vs8)?

The first invitations sent out by the son's servants were flat-out rejected. The next round-of-invitations were either ignored or incited persecution (followed by consequential judgment). Finally the banquet hall was filled with guests.

What do you suppose the "guests" represent (vs 10)?

The church

Every last detail was prepared in advance and the guests (representing the church) are gathered to the feast of the son the king loves. The king makes a glorious entrance to greet the guests when he notices someone is not properly prepared for the grand occasion (v.11).

**Was this man invited?**

Yes

**Was he properly attired?**

no

According to the customs of-the-day, the king would provide wedding garments for the guests. To not appropriate what the king provided was an extreme offense against the king, for it was to refuse rebelliously the gift of his grace.

The king made dual preparations: the feast for the guest…and the guest for the feast. There was no excuse for the guest to attend unprepared.

**Who already responded as expected in verse 15 (reference Group Three from verse 6)?**

The Pharisees respond with violence

God has prepared a wedding feast for His Beloved Son. It has been foretold in both the Old and New Testament alike.

**Read Isaiah 25:6-9.**

**For whom is this feast prepared?**

all peoples of the nation, Church Is. 2: 1-3

**Now read Revelation 19:6-9.**

**What did the apostle John see that "had come"?**

Marriage of the Lamb

**How was the Bride made ready?**

Given fine linen to wear

**What does the "fine linen" stand for?**

appropriate wedding clothes
righteous acts of saints

The invitation is extended. Preparations made.

Are ***you*** coming?

You may be prepared for *this* day, but will you be prepared for *The Day*—clothed in the garments of the Son's righteousness? Come, ready to feast... *to celebrate!*

Day 2

## What Is It That Prepares?

There have been certain seasons in my life that prepared me for some approaching life events.

For example, college prepared me for the marketplace. Similarly, Lamaze classes prepared me for childbirth. (Nothing, however, prepared me for motherhood!) Trials prepared me to encourage others. And through seasons of waiting I sought God, studied His Word, and then cultivated ways to share what I learned.

If I were to chart other examples, it might look something like this:

| Seasons of | Prepared for |
|---|---|
| Study | Teaching |
| Suffering | Ministry |
| Developing a skill | Serving and mentoring |

Ok, now it's your turn. To help prime your brain, think of the training that prepares the athlete for a competition or practice and rehearsals that prepare the performer.

What experiences have prepared you for something next?

| Seasons of | Prepared for |
|---|---|
| Practice Piano | Performing |
| Student Teaching | Teach Music Classes |
| | |

I want desperately for you to know, dear sister, that in every season—whatever that is—God is preparing you. One season prepares for the next; and on it goes. There is no season in our lives that is wasted or that cannot suit some future purpose. (But I'm getting weeks ahead of myself.)

## Ground Zero ~ How Is One Prepared?

Now let's shift our focus in order to understand the basics about preparation with regard to spiritual matters.

"Praise be to the God and Father of our Lord Jesus Christ, who has blessed us in the heavenly realms with every spiritual blessing in Christ."

(*Ephesians 1:3*)

**From Ephesians 1:3 in the sidebar, complete this sentence:**

**God** has **blessed me with** every

**spiritual blessing in** Christ.

**For clarity: Who is the Source of our every blessing?**

Christ

**Let's reiterate: We are blessed in** Christ.

**Read Ephesians 1:7-14.**

**Check the blessings we have in Christ that are mentioned in this passage:**

- ☐ **Comfort**
- ☑ **Redemption**
- ☑ **Forgiveness**
- ☐ **Riches**
- ☑ **Unity**
- ☑ **Holy Spirit**

Grace
wisdom + Understand
inheritance
hope

**What two terms does Paul use with reference to the Good News of Jesus Christ?**

**Message of** truth

**Gospel of your** Salvation

Two things—of worth beyond measure—had to be freely given for the redemption of humanity: the blood of Christ Jesus and God-gifted grace. Further blessings that stem from that redemption are the forgiveness of sins and the unification of all things to Christ. Made new and sealed by the Holy Spirit, we are lavished with grace to receive subsequent blessings from the Father, prepared to bring praise to God's glory.

Being prepared for all subsequent spiritual blessings begins with redemption.

## Now What?

Now that we've answered the spiritual questions, "Who prepares us" (God) and "How are we prepared" (redemption through Jesus Christ), what's next?

Understanding what we are now.

**Read Ephesians 2:1-22.**

**Complete the chart below. Use a 1-2 word answer in each blank, for the verse referenced in that blank, of what we were as opposed to what we are now, in Christ:**

| Were | Are Now |
|---|---|
| Vs 1) Dead | Vs 5) Alive |
| Vs 3) Child of wrath | Vs 6) Seated in heavens |
| Vs 12) Uncircumsized | Vs 13) brought near |
| Vs 14) without hope + God | Vs 16) reconciled |
| Vs 19) foreign + strangers | Vs 19) God's family |
| | Vs 22) Holy building |

Look over that amazing list one more time, my friend…as if to count your many blessings!

We *were* "dead in our transgressions and sins"; **but now** (two profound words of God's great mercy and grace), we are SAVED…RAISED…ALIVE!

What a way to end this day of our study together!

Doesn't it just make you feel ready for anything?!

## Day 3
# Preparing Temples

In the weeks ahead, we will discover more fully what God prepares *in* us, for what He has prepared *for* us. But, since in this first week we will cover the basics of preparedness, I'm going to touch lightly on this.

**Fill-in the blanks with the word *prepared*:**

**A ____________________ work**

**to do a**

**work ____________________**

We are a prepared work (prepared by God) to do a work prepared (also prepared by God).

And there are no greater illustrations of this than those found in the passages regarding the tabernacle, the temple and the church.

## Divine Building Projects

**Read Exodus 35:30-36:1.**

**According to verse 31, how were the craftsmen made able?**

________________________________________

The Hebrew word for tabernacle is *mishkan*, which means "dwelling place." (*Bible Hub*)

**The purpose was twofold. Verse 33 tells us it was "for work in every skilled craft" in building that tabernacle. Verse 34 states the other key purpose God gave these abilities:**

________________________________________

God prepared the people…to prepare others…in preparing the tabernacle, where God would dwell among His people.

**Read 1 Kings 5:1-6.**

**What had to first happen before the temple could be built, according to verse 3?**

________________________________________

**Fill in the blanks from verse 5:**

**The temple was built for the** name **of the Lord**

my **God.**

**Were sounds of iron tools heard at the temple site (6:7)?** No

**Look at 1 Kings 6:13 and choose the correct answer:**

**God promised to dwell among them, based on what condition in verse 12?**

- **A) They keep the temple clean**
- **B) As long as Solomon was king**
- **C) They obey God's commands**
- **D) Sing only David's psalms in worship**

**From verse 6:19, what was prepared for the Ark of the Covenant**

- **A) Outer courtyard**
- **B) Inner sanctuary**
- **C) Neighboring dwellings**
- **D) A cover**

**What kind of gold was used (vs 6:21)?**

- **A) 18 carat**
- **B) 24 carat**
- **C) Pure**
- **D) White**

**How many years did it take to build the temple (vs 6:38)?** 7 years

**What can we glean from these particular details about building temples?**

________________________________________

Three temple projects on Mt. Moriah were:

- Solomon's Temple
  - (960 BC-586 BC)
- Zerubbabel's Temple
  - (515 BC-20 BC)
- Herod's Temple
  - (20 BC-70 AD)

Once there was peace in the kingdom and enmity no longer abounded among the people of God, the king prepared the site and the people to build a dwelling place for the Name of the Lord.

## Redesigning Sacred Dwellings

The absence of chiseling sounds on the hardened bedrock of that ancient work is akin to the silent work of the Holy Spirit upon hardened hearts in our sanctification—sculpting temples where He dwells within His people.

Each age of the temple underwent a redesign, ultimately finishing with God's dwelling within each of us. Each redesign served the same purpose: to fill God's longing to tabernacle (originally used as both a noun and a verb in the Greek) among His creation.

"And in Him you too are being built together to become a dwelling in which God lives by His Spirit."

(*Ephesians 2:22, NIV*)

**Read Ephesians 2:19-22.**

**Match to complete the sentence.**

| | |
|---|---|
| **Built on the foundation of** | **Chief Cornerstone** |
| **With Christ Jesus as the** | **Holy temple in the Lord** |
| **And rises to become a** | **Apostles and Prophets** |

As God lavishly prepared the temples of old, He does so today.

The construction process continues. But, as we rise up together to become the holy temple of God, the church, we cannot overlook the fact that we are each a temple—the dwelling place for the glory of God.

**What work can you do on *your* temple today?**

________________________________________

I often borrow the words of hymns for prayer. Today, in closing, join me in praying these lyrics.

"O Lord, prepare me to be a sanctuary;
pure and holy, tried and true;
with thanksgiving I'll be a living sanctuary
for You."

## Day 4
# Prepared Pre-Conversion

The main profile of our study makes his grand entrance today, although I doubt he is a stranger to anyone.

Back-in-the-day, everyone knew who Saul of Tarsus was—no introduction required. He had an impressive resume, an imposing personality, and impossible pride.

The man who would be called Paul enters the biblical scene in Acts 7:58… and the Bible is never the same!

## Saul ~ The Early Years

How do you like knitting? Well, sharpen your needles; we just might need them today in knitting together the tapestry of Saul's pre-conversion life.

**Match the passage with what can be learned of Saul from it.**

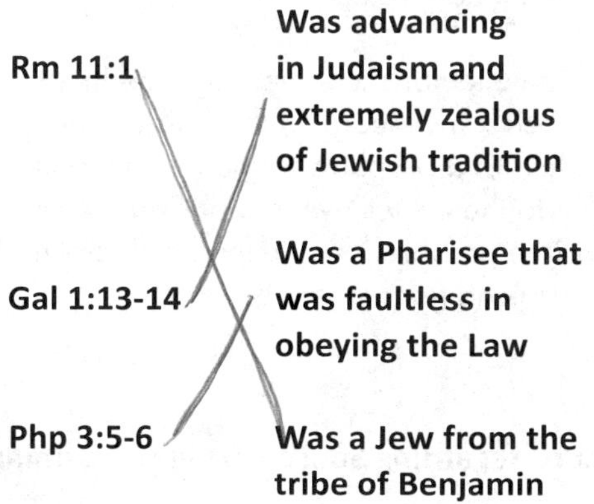


Saul, the proficient law student, could be considered a lawyer, of sorts; for he expounded, defended and prosecuted law breakers—aspiring to ascend the ruling courts of the Sanhedrin Council.

Saul was not only a Jew; he was considered a "Hebrew-of-Hebrews." He didn't fall into the classification of a Hellenistic Jew, but was an orthodox, Hebraic Jew. He would have spoken Aramaic, the language of Judea, in the home and synagogue. Scripture tells us that he had a rising reputation by zealously defending the religion of his people.

Tarsus was settled in the southeast corner of Asia Minor (now modern Turkey), in the province of Cilicia. Roughly situated about 12 miles from the Mediterranean shore, it was guarded by the Taurus mountain range. The Cilician Gate passed through the range…all the way to Rome.

**Now match what can be learned of Saul from these passages.**

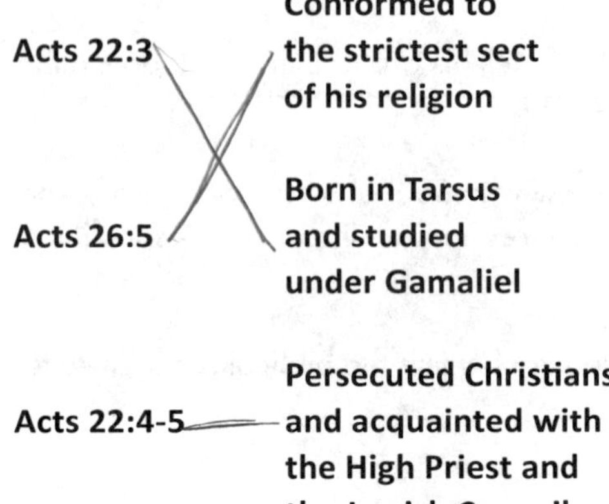


Born in the gentile city of Tarsus as the son of a Pharisee, Saul would have had the socio-economic standing and thorough education in Greek culture, literature, and language. This would serve him well in later years. He was also trained in tentmaking, preparing him to earn future income. And his Roman citizenship would have allowed for extensive travel throughout the Empire, both with privileges and legal protection.

Saul's training at the feet of Gamaliel for six years prepared him to be a master theologian. This extensive knowledge of their history, religious system, and Scriptures of the law and prophets would lay the foundation for him to reason and apply it to the New Covenant of Christ. Living the highly ritualistic life of a Pharisee prepared him to lead a disciplined and obedient life under treacherous conditions to come.

**Read Acts 7:57-8:3.**

**Complete the sentence regarding Saul's part in the stoning of Stephen.**

**"Saul** agreed **of their killing him."**

**What was happening to the church?**

growth in midst of severe persecution

**Who led the charge?** Saul + Pharisees

The time and place of his birth all played a part in preparing Saul, as did his upbringing. But all of that was about to change, as God took hold of his life for a greater purpose long prepared for him.

**Read Acts 9:1-9.**

**Write the term used in verse 1 that describes what Saul was doing.**

breathing threats 4 murder

**Who is it that stopped Saul dead-in-his-tracks?**

Christ

Jewish Christian converts fled north from Jerusalem, some 100 miles to Damascus, for refuge from persecution.

**How long did Saul sit in darkness?**

3 days

This blindness served several purposes. Ultimately, it prepared Saul to trust God, so that in all the difficulties that lay ahead, when he would not be able to see, he could press on in faith.

**Go back to Acts 9:4. What was Saul doing?**
**Yet what did he hear?**

Voice of LORD Jesus

Take that to heart, dear sister. That Voice that called out to Saul in the depths of his rebellious sin, calls out to you. There is no action so terrible that Jesus does not call you to Him from the midst of it.

Jesus Christ can change the course of our lives in a flash and set us on the path He has prepared for us. And all that lies behind—forgiven—prepared us all the way.

Day 5

# Prepared Post-Conversion

Can we ever truly be prepared for the things of God until we are in Christ?

As previously discussed, redemption is necessary to pave the way for all other spiritual blessings. We must first be right with God and reconciled to Him—and that only comes through Jesus—to be prepared to move forward in living out His will.

We learned yesterday that Paul was prepared in his early years, but only to a point. And that was used *in opposition* to God.

Paul, prior to his conversion, was headed down a clear path of destruction when Jesus called him out to follow a better Way...***Him***.

## A Change in Direction

God had something prepared for Paul. But first He had to prepare *him* for what He had prepared *for* him.

Let's continue on this journey of Paul's preparation, post-conversion.

**Each verse represents a stepping stone in Paul's timeline from his baptism to his first missionary journey. The stepping stones below are laid out on the path God would take Paul. Write the places traveled (from the Word Bank) in the blank of their corresponding stone.**

1 **Acts 9:19b-22**

2 **Gal 1:17-18**

3 **Acts 9:26-30**

4 **Gal 1:21**

5 **Acts 11:25-26**

**Word Bank:**

- **Caesarea to Tarsus**
- **Antioch**
- **Syria and Cilicia**
- **Damascus**
- **Arabia to Damascus to Jerusalem**

**What would your timeline look like? Can you also map out a path of times God has prepared you for where you are in your journey today?**

This timeline spans a period of more than 11 years in the apostle's life. This process was critical in preparing him to understand God's will, teach the gospel, and learn to follow the Holy Spirit closely.

**Read how the apostle summarizes his change in direction, from his own words recorded in Galatians 1:14-17.**

**Now match to complete each statement.**

| | |
|---|---|
| **WAS** | **he preached Christ** |
| **BUT** | **advancing in Judaism** |
| **THEN** | **he was called** |

**According to 1 Corinthians 15:10 in the sidebar, to what did Paul attribute this change?**

God's Grace

A lesson to be learned from Paul is this: Whether pre-conversion or post-conversion—before and after—we are always prepared by the grace of God.

"But by the grace of God I am what I am, and His grace to me was not without effect. No, I worked harder than all of them—yet not I, but the grace of God that was with me." (*1 Corinthians 15:10*)

## Prepared To Say

Allow me to introduce an exercise called "Prepared to Say," which we will be doing each week at the end of Day 5. Hopefully, you will find it thematic to our study from the week.

It can be used as a memory verse in the week ahead, but it is also designed to be used as an assessment tool of your faith.

The verse selected will focus on a time in which Paul had to be prepared by God in his faith to be able to make such a confident claim. Hopefully it is something we, too, are prepared to say along with Paul.

So, at the end of each week, when you reach the "Prepared to Say" section, honestly ask yourself if you are at a point in your faith where you are able to make the same statement.

Are you now prepared to say with Paul....

**Prepared to Say**

"Here is a trustworthy saying that deserves full acceptance: Christ Jesus came into the world to save sinners—of whom I am the worst. But for that very reason I was shown mercy so that in me, the worst of sinners, Christ Jesus might display His immense patience as an example for those who would believe in Him and receive eternal life" (1 Tm 1:15-16).

*WEEK TWO*

# Working the Word

Feb. 11, Tuesday

**DAY 1**

## Working Our Way to 2:10

Getting to your destination at Hartsfield-Jackson Atlanta International Airport is quite a process. There are numerous dots to connect to get where you're ultimately going.

A combination of highways and bi-ways and pathways gets you to the main terminal. Then you are shuttled along by various means of transportation that take you from terminal to concourse. A herculean escalator takes you down to an underground train, which transports you rapidly to a gliding walkway (optional, of course), depositing you at a lower level concourse. Taking another escalator or elevator ride, followed by a speedy jaunt, will eventually get you to your gate (which may or may not have been reassigned).

I got to experience all of these shuttlecrafts recently as I followed the course from one point to another, in working my way to my destination...my son.

That's our course for the day—to make our way to our destination.

And our destination? Our key verse: Ephesians 2:10.

### Too Good To Pass By

Just like I couldn't bypass any of the points on the course to my destination at the airport (except for the moving walkway); we can't skip over verses 1 through 9 of Ephesians 2.

Besides, who would want to? They are entirely too good to skip.

**Let's work our way up the word-path leading to our key verse. From Ephesians 2:1-10 of the English Standard Version below, complete the following exercises:**

In the original Greek, verses 1-10 are a single sentence.

- **HIGHLIGHT where we "once" walked and how we "once" lived.**
- **CIRCLE what we were "following."**
- **UNDERLINE the past tense suffix of what God has done in Christ, from verses 4-8.**
- **Change the pronouns "us" to "me" and "you" to "I" in verses 4-5.**

And you were dead in the trespasses and sins [2] in which you once walked, following the course of this world, following the prince of the power of the air, the spirit that is now at work in the sons of disobedience—[3]among whom we all once lived in the passions of our flesh, carrying out the desires of the body and the mind, and were by nature children of wrath, like the rest of mankind. [4] But God, being rich in mercy, because of the great love with which he loved us, [5]even when we were dead in our trespasses, made us alive together with Christ—by grace you have been saved—[6]and raised us up with him and seated us with him in the heavenly places in Christ Jesus, [7]so that in the coming ages he might show the immeasurable riches of his grace in kindness toward us in Christ Jesus. [8]For by grace you have been saved through faith. And this is not your own doing; it is the gift of God, [9]not a result of works, so that no one may boast. [10]*For we are his workmanship, created in Christ Jesus for good works, which God prepared beforehand, that we should walk in them.*

**What were we, according to verse 3?**

**Children of** ______________________________

Trespasses are infractions of the commandments of God, while sins are offenses directly against God.

**Who now rules the disobedient?**

______________________________

**How rich is God's grace in Christ Jesus (vs 7)?**

______________________________

Last week we explored what we were and are now in Christ. Now let's expand our view of the before and after of salvation.

**Draw an arrow to the correct tense of salvation.**

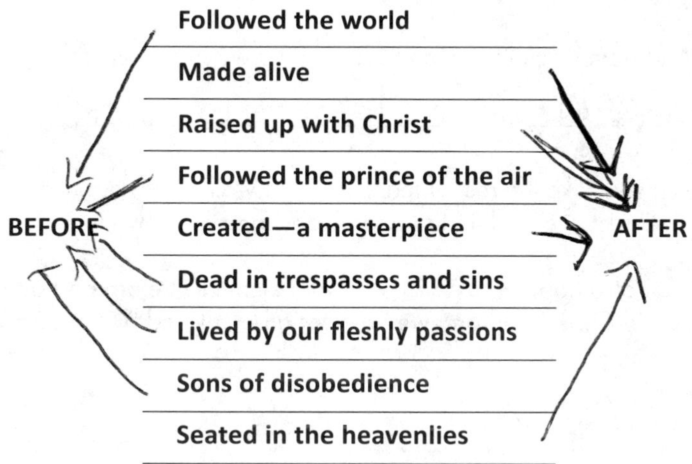


I cannot possibly overemphasize the fact that what we "once were" is **<u>past</u> <u>tense!</u>**

Neither can I fully comprehend the mercy, love, and grace of God toward us!

**What are the 2 "g's" from God in Ephesians 2:8?**

- **G** r a c e
- **G** i f t

**And Eph 2:9 further explains:**

**For salvation is not by w** o r k s

**So none can b** o a s t

Verses 1 through 3 give a glaring description of the raw material God starts with, in sinful man; verses 4 through 7 provide details of the reformation once we are in Christ—both components of the progression of the 2:10 masterpiece.

Another exciting detail I simply *must* share with you is this…

**How does Ephesians 2:1 tells us we *once* "walked?"**

sin

**And how does Ephesians 2:10 tell us we *now* "walk?"**

grace of God, good works

When we lived "like the rest of mankind," we walked in sin. But now, graced in Christ, we walk in the good works prepared by God.

But did you also happen to notice one vital element? Before and after salvation, "in Christ" and out, we have **long** been loved by God (vs 4).

## Expounding Ephesians 2:10

So, what do you do when God makes a verse come alive?

Share it!

And that's precisely what I'm going to do. (Albeit, imperfectly!)

I already shared my story behind the study in the introduction. I hadn't fully realized all God has packed into this verse, however, until I really got into the thick of study.

And, boy-oh-boy, is it ever rich!

### Capture-It in a Diagram

Diagramming sentences—you either love it…or hate it!

Will you play along? I promise it will be worth it.

**Write Ephesians 2:10.**

we are His workmanship, created in Christ Jesus for good works, which God prepared before hand, that we should walk in them

**Now, write the parts of speech, or a brief definition, or interpretive description for each of the following:**

**We** ____________________

**Are** ____________________

**God's** ____________________

**Handiwork** ____________________

**Created** ____________________

**In Christ Jesus** ____________________

**To do good works** ____________________

**Prepared** ____________________

**In advance** ____________________

**For us to do** ____________________

*For* points back...back...back to redemption—reminding us that we have no cause to boast in and of ourselves (see verses 8-9). *We* is plural and refers to all of us in Christ. *Are* is an accomplished fact—it's the verb that points to what we are. The singular, defining noun is *handiwork*—God's one-of-a-kind work-of-excellence. *God's* is possessive, for we are His... and *only* His! This masterpiece is "created," past tense, "in Christ Jesus," the God Who Saves. And this is done with purpose: to actively do good works. It answers the "why we were created in Christ." They are divinely ordained works that are common, yet varied. Corporate, yet individual. (We'll explore that more in later weeks.)

Now let's discuss the closing of this verse—those things prepared beforehand by God for us to do—because certain translations help us gain a better understanding with an added clause.

**Look up Ephesians 2:10 in the various translations noted. There are a variety of sources on the Internet. Write the ending clause to the corresponding translation below for comparison. I have provided the NIV in the sidebar.**

**ESV** ____________________

**HCSB** so that we should walk in them

**NASB** that we should walk in them

..."which God prepared in advance for us to do."

(*NIV ending of Eph 2:10*)

The NIV makes only the general statement: "for us to do." The way the verse is translated more times than not includes the phrase "that we would walk in them."

Those things God has prepared are **so that** *we would walk in them.* (Some translations state that we "**should**" walk in them.) It is as a path for us to walk. The phrase used, "that we would walk in them," is actually one Greek word—*peripatēsōmen*. It means "to walk" and refers to our conduct; the way we are to live life.

God prepared a path of good works long ago for the masterpiece He creates in Christ to walk.

And how is it that we are to walk? Well, one verse that summarizes what the Bible has to say on the matter is Deuteronomy 5:33.

**Complete the command from Deuteronomy 5:33:**

Follow the whole instruction

**to all that the Lord your God has commanded you.**

And what is the way we have been created to walk? Here is what can be learned from the Pauline epistles…

**Match the verse to the purpose of our recreation in Christ:**

| | |
|---|---|
| **Eph 1:4** | **in true righteousness** |
| **Eph 4:24** | **renewed in knowledge; in His image** |
| **Col 3:10** | **to be holy and blameless** |
| **2 Tm 2:21** | **His very own, eager to do good** |
| **Tit 2:14** | **useful instruments** |

our purpose

We have been created in Christ Jesus to reflect His image, in holiness and righteousness; to be prepared to eagerly do any good work, as useful instruments with a special purpose.

> "The conversion of a soul is a miracle of a moment, but the manufacture of a saint is the task of a lifetime."
>
> ~*Alan Redpath*

That is most remarkable. And precisely why He made us to be the masterpiece we are!

Good work today, ladies! *Keep walking!*

For we are God's workmanship, created in Christ Jesus for good works, which God prepared beforehand, that we should walk in them (ESV).

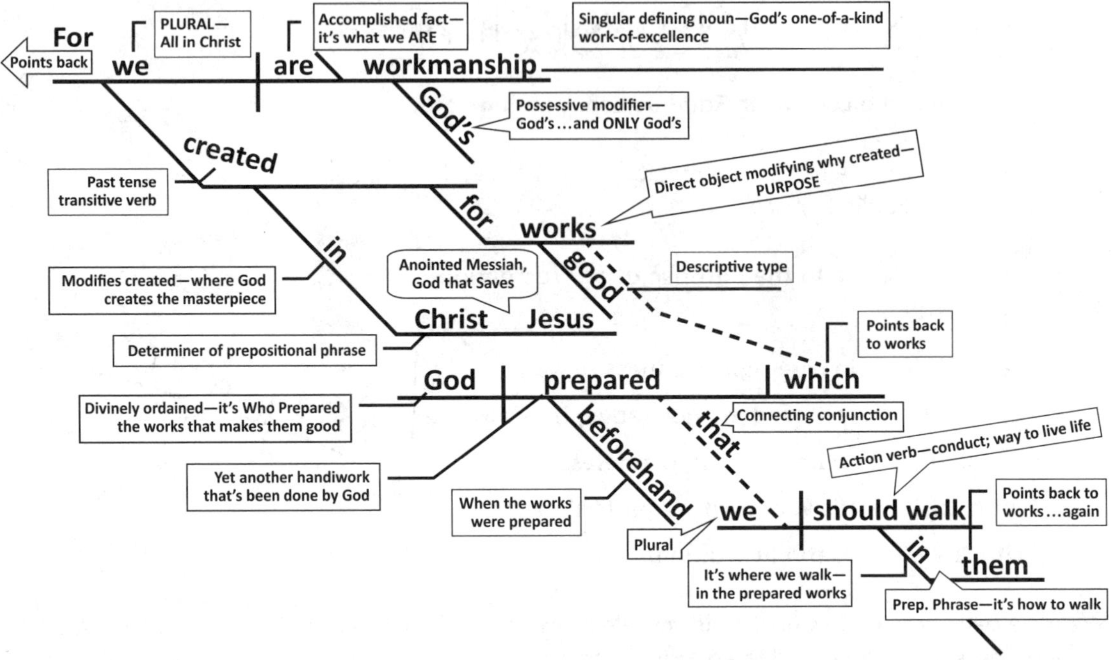


***Special shout-out of thanks to***

*Brother Jimmy Jones for his gracious literary tutoring.*

Day 3

# A Work of the Master

You've worked your way through the Word, landing on the reward of Ephesians 2:10.

(*And does God ever have something special waiting for you!*)

Let's begin at the grace that opens this verse (because doesn't *everything* begin and end with grace?!)

**Right off, the verse says that we are God's**

______________________________

**(Circle the letter that fills in the blank)**

**A. Craftsmanship**

**B. Handiwork**

**C. Masterpiece**

**D. Workmanship**

**E. All of the above**

*Poiēma*—Greek noun—meaning: "that which has been made; of the works of God as Creator." Derived from poieó — Greek verb equivalent to: "make ready; to prepare."

*NT Greek Lexicon and Strong's Concordance*

So, I want to start right there.

That is the first thing I want you to know, my friend...

**You <u>are</u> God's masterpiece!**

And the very next thing Paul writes is why that is.

**You are God's masterpiece because you are**

______________________________

What if an artist sketched your portrait?

***Then*** would you see yourself as a masterpiece?

Or would you still look at the *artwork* as the masterpiece...and not the subject itself as the real masterpiece?

From the waters of baptism God begins a work in us—

a work of grace...

a work of change...

a work to bring Him glory...

as His unique masterpiece.

**Write Isaiah 64:8.**

We are the clay, you are our Potter; we all are the works of your hands

**The masterpiece of you; what veils it? Keeps it hidden?**

**Do you see yourself as a clump of clay? Or the created work of a loving Father, made to be useful...significant... with purpose and beauty?**

## A Real Piece of Work

"Look at the world either through a telescope or a microscope and you will be dwarfed into terror by the infinitely great or the infinitely little."
*~Oswald Chambers*

I am often overcome with awe, amazement, and elation at the artistry of God's masterful creation.

And you are part of that creation—the crowning glory, image-bearing part. The part, when finished, moved Him to declare; "It is very good" (Genesis 1:31).

When I revel in the mastery of my brother Rob's art,* I am instantly filled with delight. But I, too, muse over the artistry of his life and who he has become.

* Footnote: My brother's gallery can be viewed at http://www.robingallery.com/Gallerylist.html

**What do you like to create?**

Vinyl Designs

**What creativity has God created in you?**

But aren't we *all* works-in-progress? The Bible resounds an emphatic "Yes!" to that giant question. (*And, thankfully so!*)

**From Philippians 1:6 in the sidebar, answer the following questions.**

"being confident of this, that He who began a good work in you will carry it on to completion until the day of Christ Jesus." (*Philippians 1:6*)

**How sure was Paul?**

Very, 100% confident

**What kind of work does God do?**

good

**Will He finish what He started?** Yes!

**Until when?** the day of Christ Jesus

That is one verse that is positively brimming with promise. Promise that anchors hope.

God **WILL** bring to completion the work He began in you. And He won't stop until Christ returns.

Ephesians 2:10 also speaks to purpose. The purpose we are created a masterpiece.

**Circle what is to be done with this masterpiece:**

**To be locked in a vault**

**To sit high on a pedestal**

**To earn praise**

**To do good works**

Interpreting the proper order in the structure of that verse is critical.

"By the grace of God I am what I am."
*~Apostle Paul (1 Cor 15:10)*

It is not by good works that we are created in Christ to be a masterpiece. *No!* We are in Christ by the grace of God. (No boasting, remember?)

**Look up Titus 2:14. Complete the paraphrase:**

**Jesus gave Himself to** redeem **us,**

**to purify for Himself a people for His own**

possession **who are** eager

**for good** works**.**

We become a prepared work (by His design and creation and by His saving and transforming grace in Christ) for a work prepared.

It may not be Day 5 (when we are to do our "Prepared to Say" exercise) but—right here...and right now—are you prepared to say that *you* are a masterpiece?

## Day 4
# The Unready

"Ready for anything."

You've heard the saying.

But did you know that, in Christ, you really are?

"I don't *feel* prepared," you might object (with a sudden surge of nervous fright).

How many nightmares are rooted in being caught off-guard… unprepared?

There's nothing worse than being unready—especially in matters of faith!

In fact, dare I say, it could rank right up there among the "Thou Shalt Nots."

"Thou shalt not be unready."

## A 50/50 Parable

"Unready for what," you ask?

Unready for the Lord's coming.

**Read Matthew 25:1-13.**

**Record the first three opening words of Jesus' parable:**

____________ ____________ ____________

**What does that tell you?**

"Parable means a putting alongside for purposes of comparison and new understanding."

*~Holman Illustrated Bible Dictionary* (*Published by B&H Publishing*)

That's quite a way to start a parable! It's obvious that this parable is part of a larger discourse. It must be linked to something Jesus had already said.

*Eschatos* (means last)
+ *Logos* (means word)
= *Last things*
Therefore, *eschatology* refers to the Bible's teaching regarding the end of the present age and the Messiah's return.

**Look back in the text to determine where this sermon begins. Discover the context.**

**Jesus is referring to what time?**

End of the age, or end of time

This sermon speaks to the end of this age and is delivered from the Mount of Olives. Therefore, Matthew 24-25 is known as the Olivet Discourse.

**To what is this parable compared (vs 1)?**

10 Virgins

As is invariably the case, the subject of the parable is the kingdom of heaven (referring to the reign of God through Jesus Christ).

**What equivalent would you apply to the ten virgins?**

Christians, People of God, People in General

**What is the role of a bridesmaid?**

________________________________________

Jesus uses the example of ten virgins—or bridesmaids. Isn't the responsibility of the bridesmaid to prepare the bride for the groom?

**Complete this sentence from verse 10:**

**The virgins who were** ready

**went in with him to the wedding banquet.**

**What is the instruction (vs 13; also see Mt 24:42-44)?**

Watch

**Why (see Mt 24:36, 42)?**

No one Knows the time

**Circle who is responsible for readiness (vs 9):**

**Those ready**

**Everyone else**

**The individual**

**Jesus**

You're either ready…or you aren't. And there's no one to turn to if you aren't.

This parable seems prophetic, doesn't it? Grievously, there will be those who won't be ready for Christ's coming.

obey zealously

**What determines readiness?** prepared for groom's coming

**Will you be ready?** ________

Jesus tells this parable within a succession of parables.

**What two parables follow?**

Talents - using gifts from God

Sheep & Goats - split by helping others now

**What type of parables are they?** Kingdom of heaven

**All occur when?** End of Time 2nd coming / Judgment

Jesus made it perfectly clear that judgment will accompany His return.

*Parousia*—a Greek noun—meaning: "coming" and is used in New Testament theology with regard to the second coming of Christ.

(*Strong's Concordance*)

Let's pause to pray that the percentage of the ready versus the unready far exceeds 50/50. (50/50, the ratio of the bridesmaids in the parable).

Are you like the homeowner—full of fear, dread, and anxiety that a thief will break in and you'll be caught unprepared? Or are you more like a bride—ready and waiting at the altar with a heart at peace and a gaze excitedly fixed on her bridegroom?

I pray Paul's prayer for all of us: "May God Himself, the God of peace, sanctify you through and through. May your whole spirit, soul and body be kept blameless at the coming of our Lord Jesus Christ" (1 Thess 5:23).

Day 5

# Twice Unready

Have you ever gotten ready to go somewhere only to arrive at your destination to find you aren't ready at all?

With several embarrassing examples from which to choose, I'll just pick one at random to illustrate.

It was a Sunday night, and we planned to attend a special event at church. I wanted to improve upon my usual lackluster appearance to suit the occasion. It had been a busy day, and I rushed through all the demands of the day a bit distracted. My kids were still young enough that they needed my assistance to usher them along. With the three of us ready, we rushed out the door. Once in the car, I breathed a sigh of relief that we were on time. My mind raced in several directions en route. Upon our arrival, it came to my attention that my feet were bare. We drove to the shoe store, laughing hysterically all the way. We amused the clerk with our loud tale—the kids quite entertained by my humiliation. They teased me to no end. I will never forget the lighthearted skip across the parking lot; it was a timely faux pas that broke every bit of tension I stuffed beneath that finished veneer. We sped away on the wings of joy and made it back in time for the dinner...with quite a story to tell. I may not have been ready the first time, but I sure am thankful for second chances that provide opportunities to right a wrong. I would like to report that was the only time I've done that, but it wouldn't be true. Though I haven't done it in quite some time, there was a season when all was ready...except for my feet.

**Okay, it's your turn. Share a personal story? Maybe you have one about a time you thought you were ready...but weren't?**

## A People Twice-Prepared

Let's take a little crash course in Israel's history and revisit the formative years of the nation of God.

**Read Exodus 19:1-6.**

**What is the time referenced (vs 1)?**

3 months after Exodus

**Where has God brought them (vs 2)?**

Mt. Sinai

**What was God preparing them to be (vs 6)?**

His people of priest, a holy nation

After traveling from Egypt for three months, God took His people to Mt. Sinai, His camp of preparation.

**Deuteronomy 1:2 tells us how long it takes to travel to this location:** From Sinai to Promise Land

11 days

**Read Numbers 10:11-13.**

**What is the time referenced (vs 11)?**

20th day, 2nd Month, 2nd year

**Where have they been camped (vs 12)?**

Mt. Sinai

**For *how* long?** 1 year, 11 months

**What are they doing now?**

leaving for Promised Land, wilderness of Paran

**Fill in the blank (vs 13):**

**"They set out this _____________ time...."**

Using Scripture landmarks, God delivered these people from Egypt at Exodus 12:31; they arrived at Mt. Sinai (also referred to as Horeb) at Exodus 19:1; and they camped there until Numbers 10:10.

The delivered people of God were stationed at Mt. Sinai for a whole year! During this encampment, God instructed them through the Law how to live set apart for Him. And then they were ready to travel.

**Travel Points of Numbers:**

Numbers 10:11-12:16 – From Sinai to Kadesh

Numbers 13:1-20:13 – 40 years in the wilderness of Paran and Zin

Numbers 20:14-22:1 – From Kadesh to the Plains of Moab

Numbers 22:2-36:13 – In the Plains of Moab

**Read Deuteronomy 1:6-8.**

**The Lord declared they had stayed**

long enough.

**What was God's instruction to the people?**

Journey on. Take the land as promised

**Now read the summary retold by Moses in his address recorded in Deuteronomy 1:19-40.**

**How would you paraphrase what happened next?**

12 Spies - 10 gave bad report
God refuses this generation - punished
children will get promised land

In the second year after the exodus, as recorded in Numbers 13 (and retold in Deuteronomy 1), we read that a people prepared failed to enter into the land promised of God.

They were ready to move on, to receive God's promise. But their grumbling and complaining squelched faith. Their disposition of discontentment, disobedience, disbelief, and dissatisfaction equaled disaster!

What can be learned from them?

**Discover the three "uns" that made them unready. Look up the verse and complete the "un":**

**Dt 1:26** **Unready = Un** willing

**Dt 1:32** **Unready = Un** trusting

**Nu 14:33** **Unready = Un** faithful

They then suffered the consequences of their rebellion and over the next 38 years, their descendants were prepared to inherit the promise discarded.

**Read now, from Joshua 1:1-11, about when finally they received the command to cross the river Jordan.**

God prepared a people...*twice*.

At the base of Mt. Sinai, God readied a people to advance.

They refused.

But the grace of God did not abandon them in the wilderness. He patiently waited to give them another opportunity to have the faith to make a second attempt.

And then they were ready...ready to move on.

**Have you had an instance when God readied you for something, but fear held you back—only to experience His grace that gave you a second chance to try?**

It's time for this week's *Prepared to Say*. Are you prepared to say with Paul....

**Prepared to Say**

"For it is by grace you have been saved, through faith—and this is not from yourselves, it is the gift of God" (Eph 2:8).

*WEEK THREE*

# A Matter of Circumstance

March 10, Tues

**DAY 1**

## Some Training Required

In the expanse of the Arabian Desert, Paul discerned the will of God for his life. And in the still quiet of a prison cell, he was able to discern the purpose in his tumultuous circumstances.

Paul trained in many things—discernment chiefly among them.

**How and/or when have you been able to discern that for which God is preparing you?**

**Read Galatians 1:15-17.**

**Circle the source of revelation from which Paul learned to preach Christ:**

**Apostles in Jerusalem**

**Christians in Damascus**

**God** (circled)

**Other human beings**

Arabia, in Bible times, referred to all the desert east of Israel, including the Sinai Peninsula.

Following his baptism, Paul headed to Arabia and eventually Damascus. Only after three years did he go to Jerusalem to meet with the other apostles. He attributed what he learned of Jesus and his calling to God.

**What did he discern as his divinely appointed purpose, according to what he later wrote Timothy, as recorded in 1 Timothy 2:7?**

appointed a preacher, apostle and teacher of Gentiles

You may not be able to see what God is preparing you for at this moment. Why, even Saul sat in darkness for a time. For three days he was blinded to what God was doing (Acts 9:9). But, even then, God was preparing him.

## Speaking of Discernment…

If we are going to learn what God is preparing us for and what He is preparing for us, we are in great need of discernment.

Let's search out four ways discernment is gained.

**Write out Psalm 119:125.**

I am Your servant, give me understanding so that I may know Your decrees

**This is David's** prayer **for discernment.**

**Read 1 Corinthians 2:9-16.**

**What is the Source of discernment?**

Spirit of God

**Because, with the Spirit, we have the mind of** Christ **(vs 16).**

**Fill in the blank to complete this statement from Hebrews 5:14:**

**The mature have ____________________ themselves to distinguish good from evil.**

"The wise in heart are called discerning." (*Prv 16:21a*)

"A discerning person keeps wisdom in view." (*Prv 17:24a*)

Recognizing good from evil flows out of discernment, which comes from training.

Just how do we receive that training?

The best biblical example of this being put into practice is that of the Bereans.

We must train in the skill of discernment to be able to distinguish truth, goodness, and righteousness from the imposters of this world and Satan.

Our Trainers?

- The Holy Spirit
- The Word of God
- Prayer
- Wise, godly counsel

**Read Acts 17:11.**

**What did they examine daily?**

scriptures

**Now read Proverbs 1:5.**

**Where would the discerning obtain guidance?**

listen to wise

## Discerning Our Path

The Proverbs writer has much to say about wisdom and discernment. In fact, Proverbs 14:8 states that "the wisdom of the prudent is to discern his way."

**Proverbs 4:26 cautions that we are to give careful thought to what?**

the path of ar feet

Do you remember that part of Ephesians 2:10 that says God prepared works for us in advance "that we should walk in them" (refer to Week 2, Day 2)? Well, it takes discernment to know both *how* to walk and *where* to walk along this faith-path of life.

If we are to walk in the way prepared for us, it is imperative we discern that way.

By training in discernment, we learn what God is preparing us for. Like the purpose of preaching to the Gentiles that Paul was able to discern.

Then, we must discern *how* God is preparing us—the methods and means employed for that purpose. For that, we will examine Paul's circumstances. Paul was able to discern that there was purpose in the circumstances he endured—that he might gain and share Christ.

### Day 2
# When Times Are Good

Good times.

What defines them?

Plenty? Comfort? Ease?

Quite likely, it's having a lack of want…a lack of stress…lack of pain.

Or, more concisely, it's pleasing circumstances.

> **Remember a time when everything was "good." What was it about your circumstances that made them "good"?**

It's imperative to be intentional in growing faith in times of plenty, just as it is necessary to cling to faith in times of want.

So, if "we know that in ***all things*** God works for the good of those who love him" (Rm 8:28), wouldn't that include our good circumstances?

Can't that be prime preparation time?

> **Was there something you learned in a set of good circumstances that helped prepare you for some trial that followed? Explain.**

## It's All Circumstantial

He was born in the days when Egypt's ruling Pharaoh ordered baby boys be drowned in the Nile, although his older brother somehow escaped this decree. He was brought into the palace by an Egyptian princess and "was educated in all the wisdom of the Egyptians" (Acts 7:22). He received the best instruction in the ways of their polytheistic religion of the day. Though outnumbered by slaves, the culture was becoming more and more sophisticated since the advent of chariots. Yes, life in Pharaoh's palace was the best life had to offer.

He sent Pharaoh into a murderous rage when, at 40, he fled to Midian. Though life could not compare with the luxuries of his childhood, the next 40 years of being a shepherd, husband, and father treated him well… as did his father-in-law.

All that changed when God called him from obscurity. And the life he knew—as well as his common circumstances—would never be the same. God sent him back to Egypt on a rescue mission.

A mission God had been preparing him for…when times were good.

**Who is this man?** Moses

**What in your background and/or upbringing has been put to use in a major event in your life?**

There are several similarities in the background circumstances of Moses and Paul. The early years for both could be considered "good times." And in those good times, God was preparing them for His determined plans and purposes.

**What from the following verses could be considered useful in the roles they would later fill?**

- **Acts 7:11:** Manage food during famine
- **Acts 7:22:** Education of Moses
- **Acts 7:22:** Speaking Abilities of Moses
- **Acts 22:1-3:** Education of Paul when younger

**What languages did Paul use in the conversations recorded in Acts 21:37-40?**

Greek, Hebrew

**Read Acts 22:23-29.**

**What spared Paul a flogging?**

Roman citizenship

"For I can testify about them that they are zealous for God"
(*Rm 10:2a*)

**From Romans 10:2 in the sidebar, what did Paul know about the Israelites?**

**Now, from Acts 22:3, how was it that he could relate to them?**

Paul was exactly the same

Both Moses and Paul were descendants of Abraham. Their *ethnicity* helped them better understand and relate to their fellow-man. Knowledge of the civil and religious laws and familiarity with their traditions and practices would lend tremendous aid in their future dealings.

Being raised in a higher class environment afforded them the added advantage of *education*. This education granted them the ability for intellectual discourse.

Paul was not only Jewish, but also a Roman citizen. And Moses was not only a Hebrew, but was raised in an Egyptian environment. The firsthand knowledge and *training* multiculturally and counter-culturally gained them a depth of insight to be able to debate those they would confront.

**Read 1 Corinthians 12:1-6.**

**What did Paul experience?**

______________________________________________

**But he did not ________________________________.**

Of all God's orchestrations in both Paul's and Moses' lives, those spiritual in nature were by far the best of circumstances—and those the most obvious God used to prepare them for the work He had for them to do. But they did not boast of these heavenly circumstances.

Their greatest gain from their positive circumstances was their *faith* in the sovereignty of God in directing the course of their lives. They clearly understood they were set apart from birth (Gal 1:15) and sent by God to be His servants (Ex 3:10; Gal 1:1).

God equipped and prepared these men in their favorable circumstances for use later in life—when circumstances were sure to change and become far more challenging. I've chosen to close today with a prayer borrowed from F. B. Meyer.

> *"Prepare us, O God, for all that You have prepared for us. We will not be ambitious of great things, but will walk, day by day, humbly with You, and so fulfill our course. In this way we shall become Your workmanship."*

"Then Moses said, 'Now show me Your glory.'

"And the LORD said, 'I will cause all my goodness to pass in front of you, and I will proclaim my name, the LORD, in your presence.' "

(*Ex 33:18-19a*)

**Day 3**

## When Times Are Uncertain

It was a day like any other.

He headed off to work early, having to go out of town on official business.

He neared his destination when he was suddenly cast down to the ground.

Blinding light pierced his darkness; but he needed to be kept in the dark to eventually see it.

In his waiting he wondered…and reasoned.

He spent three long, sightless days in foreign surroundings. And all those scriptures and benedictions memorized in his youth whirled on repeat—round and round his confused mind.

- It was a four to six day road trip from Jerusalem to Damascus.
- Some scholars estimate the year of the events surrounding Paul's conversion to have been about 35 AD and Paul to have been approximately 30 years old.

One thing he knew for certain: he was a man-on-a-mission, at the top of his game, when he was stopped cold in his tracks.

If only he could see! Then he could put the pieces of this bewildering puzzle together and change his circumstances.

When the scales finally fell from his eyes, he saw the light—and, eventually, the hand of God at work in his life.

Those senseless days—unable to see…*understand*—finally started to make sense.

## Turning Points

Ever been there? Stuck in the dark? Unable to see what God was doing in your life?

"All that I have seen teaches me to trust God for all that I have not seen."

*~Ralph Waldo Emerson*

**If so, explain.**

**Could God have been preparing you? If so, how?**

In your waiting and wondering, do you tend to worry?

When my nephew, Mitchell, found himself waiting to start a new job, his wise Aunt Yvonne remarked, "Channel your worry into preparedness."

In your waiting, don't worry—trust. More specifically, trust God.

God is pleased when we choose to trust Him in our waiting.

What else can be done in our waiting?

**Psalm 5:3 tells us what David did in his waiting:**

Prayed

**What is the instruction given in Colossians 3:1-2?**

Seek things above

**How are we transformed to know God's will according to Romans 12:2?**

present bodies as living sacrifice

**Isaiah 50:10b**

"Let the one who walks in the dark, who has no light, trust in the name of the LORD and rely on their God."

When we can't see what God is doing or why—especially in bewildering circumstances—it is imperative to keep trusting, keep praying, keep seeking, and keep renewing our minds with God's Word.

**Read Acts 9:1-9.**

**Retell the event in your own words:**

**Read a parallel of this in Acts 22:3-11.**

**What other details does Paul give?**

Turning Point–noun: "The point at which a very significant change occurs; a decisive moment; a moment when the course of events is changed."

(*Free Dictionary, n.d.*)

Typically, the conditions changed are beyond your control to change them. Often circumstances change from good to challenging, where you are left wondering about the uncertainty of it all.

Paul's life was about to take a new and quite different direction. But it crashed head-on with the Risen Lord to prompt that change.

Paul may not have realized it at the time, but those days crouched in blindness proved to be a major turning point in his life.

Let's look at just a few other turning points recorded in Scripture.

**What was the turning point for the prodigal son from Luke 15:16-20?**

so hungry to eat pigs food

**What was the turning point for Peter from John 21:3-9?**

Saw risen Messiah

**What did Job's realization bring about, as recorded in Job 42:5-6?**

repentence

"If you want to hear God's voice clearly and you are uncertain, then remain in His presence until He changes that uncertainty."

*~Corrie ten Boom*

Sometimes uncertain circumstances are meant to bring about a turning point. For Paul, that turning point was repentance.

**To what did that repentance lead, as penned in Galatians 2:20?**

live in Christ by faith

Paul was "crucified with Christ." And once he set his sights on Christ Crucified, he saw all things in a new and glorious light. His life took a new direction…with a new mission.

But first he needed to experience a turning point—and that included a stint of uncertain circumstances.

It was far from the last time Paul would need to trust God in his waiting. But those three days prepared Paul in ways that would prove useful later. There were circumstances in his future for which God was preparing him—times when he would rely on faith when he couldn't see the way ahead.

When you can't see what God is doing—and things just don't make sense—consider the possibility that this might be a turning point where God is preparing you for a future greater good.

Day 4

## When Times Are Hard

One sure means of growth God uses is hard circumstances. And hardships are the topic-of-focus for today. (*I'll try to be gentle.*)

Now, mind you, there are varying degrees of difficult circumstances but I think you will agree that it is different than all-out suffering, which we will discuss in the coming weeks.

Why, just in reflecting upon recent weeks, I can find an example that might help explain this point further. I recently had to take my athletic son to the orthopedic specialist for a sports-related injury. The doctor diagnosed him with a fibula stress fracture. Now, that is sure to make his life rather challenging for the next several weeks as it heals. But that does not compare to the suffering I read of in the headlines of the persecuted Christians in northern Iraq fleeing for refuge from ISIS. That is outright suffering!

Circumstances change; **BUT**: "Jesus Christ is the same yesterday and today and forever." (*Heb 13:8*)

Difficult circumstances can come from myriad fronts, but they don't have to shake faith. In fact, in the midst of difficult circumstances, we can allow God to mature faith.

In every circumstance, God is there...to prepare. We don't always know for *what* He is preparing us, however, until we're either smack-dab in it or way past it. So, we must live in the moment—fully aware of present opportunities that He gives us—discerning a proper response to the situation.

### When Hard Can Be Good

Arduous was the journey; rugged the terrain.

Each challenge prepared Paul for the next.

And each difficulty called upon the grace of God for strength, discernment and endurance.

Time and again God showed up—proving He could be trusted...relied upon to be faithful.

And that's just the point of truth Paul tried to stress in his letters to the newfound churches.

"Circumstance"—
from two words:

Circum – Stance
↓ ↓
Circle + Stand

It is to be encompassed; surrounded. To stand encircled by an issue… as in: "hard-pressed on every side."

(*See 2 Cor 4:8*)

**Read 2 Corinthians 11:22-33.**

**What were some of the situations confronted that made things hard for Paul (remember, not those that inflicted downright suffering)?**

traveling frequently
threats of dangers
sleepless nights - weary

**What could they be working in him?**

**What was Paul willing to do for the gospel?**

everything

**What about you?** ____________________

**Did difficult circumstances defeat Paul?**

**Do they need defeat you?** ______________

**Why not?**

Paul labored extensively for the church. He was burdened with concern for the new converts and the opposition they faced. He lived the hard life of a nomad, often being hunted down. He stated that he was sleep-deprived, cold, and naked.

**Do you think that experiencing hardship may have helped to prepare him for a more difficult one to follow?**

Paul also endured three shipwrecks and was frequently (and unjustly) imprisoned. With each difficulty I believe he discovered more of the immutable nature and character of God—learning He could be unequivocally trusted.

Epistles written while Paul was imprisoned in Rome:

- Ephesians
- Philippians
- Colossians
- Philemon

**Fill-in the blanks from Psalm 118:5-6:**

**"When** hard pressed**, I cried to** the LORD**; He brought me into a spacious place.**

**The Lord** is with me**;**

**I will not** be afraid**."**

And there is something else Paul learned in his hardships: though times are tough there are certain things we can know.

**What were truths Paul knew about God that you can know, too? Match the truth with its verse:**

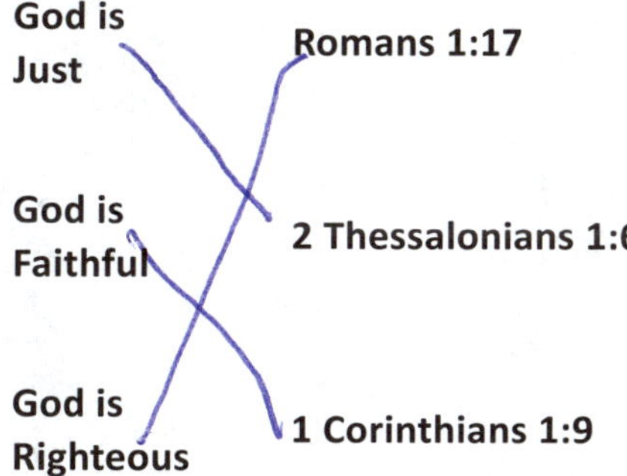


**And there are facts we can know about our faith when times are hard. Match the truth with its verse:**

| | |
|---|---|
| **God is for you** | **1 Corinthians 12:5** |
| **Christ is in you** | **Ephesians 1:19-20** |
| **His Power for you** | **Romans 8:31** |

In difficult circumstances, turn to the things you can know and rely upon, by turning to the truths in God's Word. Like these reassuring words from Psalm 71:19-21:

*"Your righteousness, God, reaches to the heavens,*
*You who have done great things.*
*Who is like You, God?*
*Though You have made me see troubles,*
*many and bitter,*
*you will restore my life again;*
*from the depths of the earth*
*You will again bring me up.*
*You will increase my honor*
*and comfort me once more."*

Day 5

# Opposed & Rejected

Before we delve into study today, let's recap our week…

We first looked at the importance of discernment regarding the ins and outs of preparedness. And we have seen that quite often the "how God is preparing us" is through our changing circumstances—whether good, hard, or uncertain.

Difficult circumstances do much to grow and refine us. And what more difficult circumstance is there than opposition?

Borrowing yet again from the life of Paul, today we will see how the rejection and opposition he experienced made him a more trusting—and determined—servant.

## When the Crowd's Against You

Paul may have gained many converts to Christ Jesus, but he sure roused dissension among the crowds simply by preaching the gospel.

**Read Acts 13:44-52.**

**Circle the correct answer to the following:**

**Who were those gathered (vs 44)?**

**A few Jews**

**A group of Gentiles**

**Almost the whole city**

**Roman guards**

**For what purpose were they gathered (vs 44)?**

**To vote**

**To hear the word of the Lord**

**To celebrate a holy feast**

**To worship**

**Who does verse 45 say was "jealous"?**

**The Gentiles**

**The Jews**

**Barnabas**

**The women**

**What was the crowd's response (vs 45)?**

**They quietly listened**

**They treated them with respect**

**They had them arrested**

**They abused them**

**What did Paul and Barnabas determine to do (vs 46)?**

turn to Gentiles - as God commanded

"And the disciples were filled with joy and with the Holy Spirit."

(*Acts 13:52*)

**Despite their persecution, what was the disposition of the Christians according to verse 52 in the sidebar?**

joy

**Read the following two passages and note the hot topics that riled opposition from the crowd:**

- **Acts 18:12-13** ____________________
- **Acts 19:23-27** ____________________

Everywhere they went, Paul and Barnabas faced opposition and rejection from Jew and Gentile alike.

As did Jesus.

**According to Luke 6:22, what does Jesus call the rejected?** ____________

**Fill in the blanks from Luke 10:16:**

**Ultimately, those who reject you, reject __________.**

**And those who reject Jesus, reject ______________.**

**Finally, read Paul's words to Christians in 2 Thessalonians 1:4-10. He told them that their perseverance in the face of persecution made them worthy of**

the Kingdom of God

**What words of encouragement does he give in verses 6-10 that may help you?**

He gives relief @ judgment
We will glorify and marvel at Him

"With this in mind, we constantly pray for you, that our God may make you worthy of His calling, and that by His power He may bring to fruition your every desire for goodness and your every deed prompted by faith. We pray this so that the name of our Lord Jesus may be glorified in you, and you in Him, according to the grace of our God and the Lord Jesus Christ."

(*2 Thess 1:11-12*)

The actions and opinions of the crowd never swayed Paul. He never quit—but pressed on…to finish strong.

And by the power of the very same Holy Spirit you can, too!

There was nothing in Paul's life—or ours—that God could not use to prepare for His plans and purposes.

It does, however, come down to a choice in attitude—in how one chooses to respond to those circumstances.

Paul conveyed God's teaching of two attitudes we are to have—*no matter our circumstances.*

**Note what those two attitudes are.**

**Philippians 4:11** Contentment

**1 Thessalonians 5:18** rejoice thankfulness

**Does your life demonstrate a faith that God can be trusted—and is to be praised—in all circumstances?**

In closing out this week, I'll ask you one more question:
In ***all*** circumstances, are you prepared to say with Paul…

### Prepared to Say

"But whatever were gains to me I now consider loss for the sake of Christ" (Php 3:7).

WEEK FOUR

# Prepared By

**DAY 1**

## Divine Encounters

In my years in the Lord's church, I have been blessed by the ministry staff of two home congregations. The staff at both locations are the true church leaders Jesus intends for His church. Among all the other godly qualities they possess and the roles they fill with complete commitment, they have been accessible, relational, and crucial in my equipping and growth. The gracious gift of God to me—and the Lord's church—through them is extraordinary.

I have been privileged to receive the preaching and teaching of godly men like Ray Hawkins, Bill Long, Don McLaughlin, and Ken Snell. And the list goes on. I've been blessed to have been mentored by Gary Horn, Jeff Kenee, Sid Bloomer, Scott Franks, and Mike Sparks.

There have been others...many others. And there have been countless lay people in the church, fellow saints, all of whom have made contributions in the process of preparation.

## A Plan of Perfection

I single out church leaders, however, because they are the ones spoken of by Paul in today's text.

**Read Ephesians 4:11-16.**

**Who is the Giver (vs11)?** ____________________

**Something given is called a** ____________________.

**From verse 11, list what Christ gave.**

______________________________________________

______________________________________________

______________________________________________

______________________________________________

Ephesians 4:11-16 is one sentence in the original Greek. Other long sentences of Paul's in Ephesians are

- 1:3-14
- 1:15-23
- 2:1-7
- 3:1-13
- 3:14-19
- 4:1-7
- 6:14-20

( *The Bible Knowledge Commentary New Testament* )

**What are those gifts?**

**Gifted Church Leaders**

**Speakers**

**Event Coordinators**

**Program Directors**

**Why were they given? Their objective is two-fold. Fill in the blanks from verse 12.**

**To** ______________________________

**For** ______________________________

**So that** ______________________________

Verse 12 is translated in the American Standard Version as "the perfecting of the saints." The Greek word used is *katartismon*, which means: a preparing or perfecting.

(*Bible Hub, n.d.*)

The gift of Christ Himself to the church is its leaders. The apostles and prophets may not be with us anymore, but they laid the foundation being built upon by the others. Though they are no longer here in the body, we can still be equipped by their inspired work.

The other God-given leaders are trainers, of sorts. They train and equip people for a specific purpose: works of service. Their purpose is the preparing or perfecting of the saints. (Compare your version to other translations or refer to a Greek lexicon for further study.) They administer the Word to the saints so they, in turn, can minister to others. And that is just the perpetual giving-economy of Jesus.

"In Him the whole building is joined together and rises to become a holy temple in the Lord."

(*Ephesians 2:21*)

**Look again at Ephesians 4:13, and state the mutual goal.**

______________________________

______________________________

**We are to reach unity and become**

______________________________

**Circle the standard of that maturity:**

**Once I reach my own personal goals**

**Sometimes have Christ-like character**

**I'm mostly like Christ in some areas**

**Whole measure of the fullness of Christ**

The use of "unity" here does not refer to a union (as in being united) but points more toward uniformity—in having one-and-the-same faith.

Those given by Christ train the saints, to serve and build the Body, until **we all** grow to maturity. That maturity occurs when the whole Body has reached completeness, to the full measure of Christ.

**How long do you suppose that takes?**

**What reasons are given in verse 14 for this necessity?**

______________________________________________

______________________________________________

God wants to protect His children from being easily tossed around by false teaching or duped by man's scheming deceitfulness.

**Finally, what is the result stated in Ephesians 4:16?**

______________________________________________

**This happens how (see verse 15)?**

______________________________________________

All the integral parts of the body, properly joined in Christ, will build and grow to edify itself in love. What better result can there possibly be?

God's plan for the Lord's church is, indeed, one of perfection.

The leaders in your home congregation are divine gifts given to grow and prepare you. And those serving alongside you are divinely gifted to build up the church. Shouldn't we then consider our encounters as divine ones?

**Who have been your spiritual trainers?**

______________________________________________

______________________________________________

**What is our instruction found in Hebrews 13:7?**

______________________________________________

My closing prayer for us today is taken from Hebrews 13:21:

*May God "equip you with everything good for doing His will, and may He work in us what is pleasing to Him, through Jesus Christ, to whom be glory forever and ever. Amen."*

Day 2

## Agents of Preparation

Let me show you where we are headed in our study for the next few weeks. As means of explanation, this should give direction and help clarify some of the prepositions I've assigned.

| | |
|---|---|
| Prepared By | **Agents** we are prepared by |
| Prepared In | **Experiences** we are prepared in |
| Prepared For | **Future things** we are prepared for |
| Prepared To | How we are to **act and respond** |

Yesterday I introduced things we are **prepared by** with our lesson on leaders in the church. We will continue studying other agents we are prepared by, such as faith, the Holy Spirit, prayer and the Word, and fellow saints.

## Progressing from Believing to Remembering

Think for a moment of the faith we have man-to-man, like the person crossing a bridge traveling to work believes in the ironworkers' workmanship. The patient believes the pharmacist to measure out the correct ingredients in filling the doctor's orders. The bank client believes the system operator will complete the payment process on his auto-draft. And the employee trusts her employer to mail in the tax and insurance check. All of these believe without reasonable assurance of their integrity of character and track record.

That's a lot of faith. But not faith that saves! Glorious saving faith comes only by Christ Jesus and the great grace of God.

How much greater, then, should our faith be in an infallible God of all perfection and goodness?

**Use your own words to translate Hebrews 11:6:**

___

___

___

**What remark did Jesus make to the woman in Matthew 9:22?**

______________________________________________

______________________________________________

It is impossible to please God without faith. Matthew 9:22 is but one example of how Jesus commended faith at every turn.

And the apostle Paul?

**From Galatians 2:20 in the sidebar we learn that the life Paul lived, he lived**

______________________________________________ .

"The life I now live in the body, I live by faith in the Son of God, Who loved me and gave Himself for me."
(*Galatians 2:20b*)

**Let's see how God prepares us by faith. Look up each verse noted and fill in the blank.**

**Acts 26:18** **We are ______________________ by faith**

**Gal 2:16** **We are justified by ______________________ not by______________________**

Faith—it's the essential starting point from whence everything else flows. By God's grace, we are first prepared by faith to grow in faith. Then, as it is active, it is an agent God uses to prepare us.

**Look up each verse and note how God continues to prepare us by our faith.**

**1 Pt 1:5** **We are ______________________ through faith by God's ______________________ ______________________**

**2 Tm 3:15** **We are made ______________________ for salvation through faith**

Pure faith invites the transforming power of God into our lives.

**Read Galatians 3:1-5.**

**What problem was Paul addressing?**

____________________________________________

It all begins with believing. And, as discovered from the above passage, it must remain so.

Let's review the life of Abraham as an example.

**Read Romans 4:18-25.**

**Did Abraham "weaken" in his faith (vs 19)?**

**Did he waver (vs 20)?**

**Instead, he "________________________ in his faith**

**and gave glory to God" (vs 20).**

Like Abraham, we must keep believing. For that, faith must be exercised. And it is exercised by remembering.

"Faith is to believe what you do not yet see; the reward for this faith is to see what you believe."
*~Augustine of Hippo*

**According to Psalm 106:12, what did the Israelites do?**

____________________________________________

**But then what happened, as recorded in the next verse (Ps 106:13)?**

____________________________________________

Spiritual forgetfulness is an enemy to our faith. It is imperative we remember both what God has promised us and what He has done for us—lest we forget and lose faith.

We must remember. Remember the cross of Christ and the grace of God. This sort of remembering is a discipline practiced purposefully.

**How can faith be exercised in remembering?**

**What are you doing now to exercise faith?**

If faith is exercised and active, it thrives and grows and produces love (1 Tm 1:5) and good deeds (Jas 2:22).

We are first prepared for the sanctifying work of God through the Holy Spirit by believing. And we are further prepared by faith in continually remembering the gospel of grace.

Continuing to believe and remember opens the door for God to work in preparing and perfecting our salvation—making faith an agent by which we are prepared.

Day 3

# The Work of the Spirit

We have a big topic to tackle today (one that could easily be an entire study itself!), so let's jump right in.

**Note the role of the Holy Spirit as told in**

- **2 Thessalonians 2:13** ____________________
- **1 Peter 1:2** ____________________
- **Titus 3:5-6** ____________________

"All the divine attributes ascribed to the Father and the Son are equally ascribed to the Holy Spirit. The Holy Spirit is a person, the Third Person of the Trinity...He is not a vague, ethereal shadow, nor an impersonal force."

*~Bill Bright*

The definition of the Greek word for sanctification in Strong's Concordance is "the process of making or becoming holy." But I especially like the definition given in *HELPS Word Studies*: "the believer progressively being transformed into the Lord's likeness."

The Holy Spirit has several roles, like counselor and convictor (Jn 16:7-8), teacher and reminder (Jn 14:26), leader and guide (Acts 8:29), helper and intercessor (Rm 8:26), and encourager (Acts 18:9). Among all these are the tasks of sanctifying and renewing those saved in Christ.

## The Holy Spirit and Paul

Paul was prepared by the Holy Spirit at every turn. He recorded several occasions in which the Holy Spirit prepared him for what was to come in his work for the Lord. They will be our main focus of study.

**Read Acts 16:6-10.**

**The missionary team was kept from traveling into Asia**

**by ______________(vs 6).**

**What occurred when they went to Mysia (vs 7)?**

____________________

**What happened that night in Troas (vs 9)?**

____________________

**Complete Acts 20:22:**

**"And now, ______________________ by the Spirit, I am going to Jerusalem."**

**What are a few synonyms for *compelled?***

______________________________________________

______________________________________________

**Have you ever felt the urgings of the Holy Spirit? If so, explain.**

______________________________________________

______________________________________________

______________________________________________

**According to Acts 20:23 what did the Holy Spirit do for Paul? ______________________________________**

**Read Acts 21:3-14.**

**From verse 4, how were the disciples able to warn Paul?**

______________________________________________

**The Holy Spirit delivered a message for Paul through Agabus. What was it?**

______________________________________________

______________________________________________

**He was better armed with this message, but was he dissuaded? ________**

Beyond these occurrences that mention help from the Holy Spirit, what I find fascinating are the visions he also received "from the Lord" (Acts 18:9; 23:11), and "an angel of God" (Acts 27:23).

With every experience, Paul grew in knowledge, faith, and confidence in the Lord. And he shared what he learned.

**Here is one example from 1 Corinthians 2:9-12.**

**Who knows the mind of God (vs 11)?**

____________________________________________

**Fill in the blank from verse 9:**

**The Spirit reveals what God has __________________ for those that love Him.**

**How are we able to understand what God has given us (vs 12)?**

____________________________________________

It is not by human knowledge or experience that we come to know what God has prepared for us. It is revealed by the Spirit. Therefore, we must abide in the Spirit—"keep[ing] in step with the Spirit" (Gal 5:25).

Paul instructed believers in his epistle to the Ephesians to "be filled with the Spirit" (Eph 5:18). This is in the present passive imperative form. I'll break that down. The present tense in the Greek is a continuous action. The passive voice signifies that it is something done to the subject. The imperative means that it is a command. To sum that all up: it is a command to be continually repeated.

"As a body without breath is a corpse, so the Church without the Spirit is dead."

*~John R. W. Stott*

Paul labored by the Spirit's energy (Col 1:29) and was guided, warned, and led by the Spirit. And his faith was prepared by the Holy Spirit to maturity. He earnestly prayed for power through the Spirit in the believer so that Christ might dwell within them through faith (Eph 3:14-19).

This is one prayer that bears repeating…often.

Day 4

# Two Powerful Agents of Change

We have seen how Christ-followers are prepared by faith and the Holy Spirit. Today we will unpack how we are also prepared by two other powerful agents—prayer and the Word of God.

## First Up: Prayer

Oh, the things God has provided as a means to prepare us in discipleship! And one of the most dynamic is prayer.

Let's start with the basics and move on from there.

**Circle the truth found in 1 Peter 3:12 from the sidebar.**

**God sometimes hears our prayers**

**God tunes-out our prayers**

**God hears and attends to our prayers**

"For the eyes of the Lord are on the righteous and His ears are attentive to their prayer..."
(*1 Peter 3:12a*)

**Read a portion of Hannah's plight recorded in 1 Samuel 1:4-18.**

**Select who was better able to comfort her and help her in her situation:**

**Elkanah**

**Peninnah**

**Eli, the Priest**

**The Lord**

**Did she mask her feelings in prayer?**

**Look ahead to verse 20. Did God grant her the desire of her heart?**

"We hear it said that 'Prayer alters things'; prayer not so much alters things as [it] alters the man who prays...The essential meaning of prayer is that it nourishes the life of the Son of God in me and enables Him to manifest Himself in my mortal flesh."

~*Oswald Chambers*
The Quotable Oswald Chambers (McCasland)

**Turn now to Acts 7:59. Who did Stephen turn to for help in his time of great need?**

Elkanah could not comfort Hannah. Peninnah could not help (*she was part of the problem*). Eli could give her no peace. No one could change her situation but God. Stephen also knew there was no one else to whom he could turn for help in his situation. Their faith knew of the sovereignty of God. A sovereignty that encompasses the externals...and beyond.

**Read James 5:17-18.**

**Can prayer move God to change things externally?**

**Read Psalm 40:1-3.**

**Can prayer move God to change things personally?**

**Through prayer, did the psalmist move from a cry of desperation to one of peace and confidence? So then, does prayer change things internally?**

This psalm is but one of many prayers in which the psalmist is obviously moved from a desperate plea to songs of praise and thanksgiving. There are several prayers recorded in the Book of Psalms where a noticeable change from distress to confidence occurs, proving God also changes things within through prayer. There is no better example of this in the New Testament than that of our Lord Jesus in the Garden of Gethsemane.

**Read Mark 14:35-36.**

**Did Jesus' circumstances change?**

**Did His resolve?**

I recall times when I began a prayer asking God to remove a hardship and then was moved to pray that He make me strong enough to endure it. In those times, I can undoubtedly affirm that God has prepared me... through prayer.

We are prepared by prayer; sometimes by a change in the externals, but always by a change internally—in gaining renewed strength, renewed hope, and renewed trust.

## Prepared by The Word

The Word of God is also a means by which God can grow us in faith and character.

**What can you ascertain from Isaiah 55:11 about God's Word?**

________________________________________

________________________________________

**According to 1 Thessalonians 2:13, what does God's Word do in the believer?**

________________________________________

________________________________________

**Read Psalm 119:97-104.**

**Match but a few of the benefits of abiding in God's Word:**

| | |
|---|---|
| **Verse 98** | **I gain understanding** |
| **Verse 100** | **God Himself teaches me** |
| **Verse 101** | **It makes me wise** |
| **Verse 102** | **I learn the right path** |

"And we also thank God continually because, when you received the word of God, which you heard from us, you accepted it not as a human word, but as it actually is, the word of God, which is indeed at work in you who believe."

(*1 Thessalonians 2:13*)

The Word of God is powerful to bring about change and active in accomplishing God's purposes. And it is an agent God has provided to bring about transformation and maturity in Christ's disciples.

Prayer and God's Word do a far greater work than change our circumstances. Both bring about a change in perspective that realigns our will to God's will. They bring about a change of heart on a matter—any matter—to what *really* matters...the eternal things of God in Christ Jesus.

Day 5

## God's Work Through Others

Have you ever crossed paths with someone and felt afterward that the encounter was heaven-sent?

I have experienced instances when words spoken in passing were just what I needed to hear, at the precise time I needed to hear them. I have been encouraged in my faith and work for the Lord unbeknownst to the other person. Through the work of Christ, they were providing what I was lacking and helped me to grow stronger and carry on.

### The Blessing of Others

God often prepares us by way of others. And the Bible is rife with such accounts.

The name Ananias is derived from the Hebrew name "Hananiah," which means "God is gracious."

**Read Acts 9:10-19.**

**Ananias is referred to as a (vs 10):**

______________________________

**What does verse 11 say Saul was doing?**

______________________________

**How was the Lord preparing him of what to expect**

**(vs12)?** ______________________________

**What concern did Ananias express, according to his response recorded in verses 13-14?**

______________________________

**From Saul's mission stated in Acts 9:1-2, was this a valid**

**concern?** __________

**What purpose did the Lord have in using Ananias (vs 15-16)?**

______________________________________

**What term did Ananias use in addressing Saul (vs 17)?**

______________________________________

**What was the result of Ananias's *Yes***

**(vs 17-19)?**______________________________

______________________________________

The Lord Jesus appeared to Saul on the Damascus road (Acts 9:3-5). He could have brought about the same result in Saul without any assistance. But He chose to use one of His disciples in the life of another. Though reluctant at first, Ananias ultimately was obedient to the Lord's "Go!" (Acts 9: 15).

**Have you ever experienced a time when you had reservations about doing something you felt God was leading you to do? Explain.**

______________________________________

______________________________________

______________________________________

Thankfully, Ananias said *Yes!*

The message Ananias delivered helped Saul understand the will of God and plans for his life (see also Acts 22:12-16).

This is just one instance when Saul was prepared by others. The one valuable lesson he learned—and exemplified—was to then actively prepare others in their walk.

**Read 1 Thessalonians 3:1-10.**

**Why did Paul dispatch Timothy (vs 2)?**

______________________________________

"Fellow-worker"=
*sun + ergos*
"Sun" means "together with; joined closely; in tight identification."
Do you have any "fellow-workers" you can name?

**What were the Thessalonians experiencing (vs 3)?**

________________________________________

**Circle the correct statement Paul made from verse 3 regarding trials:**

**We are destined for them**

**We are exempt from them**

**We should never expect them**

**From verse 5, what was Paul's other fear for their faith?**

________________________________________

The Greek word translated as "supply" in the NIV of 1 Thes 3:10 is *katartisai*. It is also used in Eph 4:12 and translated in the NIV as "to prepare."

**What was his prayer (vs 10)?**

________________________________________

Paul provided for their encouragement to better prepare them to endure trials and temptation—something every Christian can expect.

But what does this preparing of others look like? See Paul's elaboration of how he dealt with the Christians in Thessalonica.

**Read 1 Thessalonians 2:7-12.**

**What stands out to you?**

________________________________________

________________________________________

________________________________________

God uses His saints in the lives of others. And He may need to use any one of us at any given time.

Be ready!

God has employed several means by which we are prepared spiritually, so that we may live a vibrant and God-glorifying life.

Those we have identified this week are all necessary and are made available to us all by God's abundant grace.

And it all begins will the ability to say, with Paul...

**Prepared to Say**

"I have been crucified with Christ and I no longer live, but Christ lives in me. The life I now live in the body, I live by faith in the Son of God, who loved me and gave himself for me" (Gal 2:20).

*WEEK FIVE*

# Prepared In

**DAY 1**

## Experiences for Preparation

Childhood and the northern woodlands of Michigan make for a great combination. I loved all the fun adventures we had in the great outdoors… except one. I can't say I entirely enjoyed working in our vegetable garden. I did learn a lot, however.

When harvest time came every autumn, the canning and freezing marathon began. We made jams, jellies, and a variety of fruits and vegetables (*talk about hard work!*).

Whenever I smell a pickle, I remember the 20-gallon pickling crock we had for our fresh-from-the-garden cucumbers. I assure you: There is no other way to prepare a pickle unless it's first dipped in brine.

Some things are best created after they've been *in* something. Like pottery in an oven, a pearl in an oyster, or cucumbers in brine.

### The Blessing of Crucibles

Do you recall our study of Paul's circumstances from 2 Corinthians 11:22-33 during Week Three? On Day 4 we dove into the matter of hard times. This week, we are taking "hard" and heaving it up to another level of discomfort. We will revisit that passage, as well as look at several new ones, to witness how Paul experienced every level of "difficult" that exists.

"We do not want you to be uninformed, brothers and sisters, about the troubles we experienced in the province of Asia. We were under great pressure, far beyond our ability to endure, so that we despaired of life itself."
(*2 Corinthians 1:8*)

**Fill in the blanks from 2 Corinthians 1:8 in the sidebar:**

**We do not want you to be**

______________________________

**about the** ______________________________

**we** ______________________________.

**They were under great** ______________________________

"Great pressure" from the NIV is translated in other versions as: weighed down exceedingly (ASV); crushed and overwhelmed (NLT); utterly burdened (ESV); burdened excessively (NASB). You get the point, right?

**Re-read 2 Corinthians 11:23-28 to refresh your memory with the things Paul suffered.**

Paul experienced great suffering, indeed! But what else did he experience?

**Read 2 Corinthians 1:3-7.**

**Paul shared what Christ provides in suffering.**
**Circle the correct statement that correlates to verse 5:**

**In sharing in Christ's sufferings, through Christ, they also shared in His comfort.**

**As the suffering of Christ flowed into their lives, they were left to suffer alone.**

**As they shared abundantly in the suffering of Christ, comfort decreased through Christ.**

Paul stated unequivocally that as their suffering abounded, so, too, the comfort of Christ abounded. He expounds the mercy of God—in that, while they may have suffered, it was only to a point. It was never more than they could handle or beyond their ability to endure, for it was always coupled with the comfort of God's grace.

**Read 2 Corinthians 4:8-9.**

**Take this principle and personalize it. List an affliction you've experienced in your life. Next to it write a "but not" statement of how bad it could have been, but wasn't.**

__________________ **but not** __________________

__________________ **but not** __________________

__________________ **but not** __________________

The Holy Spirit always kept Paul's perspective in proper alignment. No matter what he suffered, he was keenly aware of the presence and grace of God—the same grace is available to you and me.

**Do you have to feel good to feel blessed? Explain:**

________________________________________

________________________________________

**Do you have to feel comfortable to feel content? Explain:**

________________________________________

________________________________________

"Everything can be taken from a man but this one thing, the last of human freedoms: to choose one's given attitude in any set of circumstances. Where they could take away from me all things—my clothing and my food and my comfort—but this one thing they could not take from me: my power to choose how I would respond. That is something no one can take from me."

~*Viktor Frankl*

**Read Philippians 4:11-13.**

**How have you experienced the strength of Christ to endure trials?** ____________________________

________________________________________

________________________________________

**Now look to 2 Corinthians 6:4-10.**

**They "commended" themselves in every way because they were** ____________________ **of God.**

**What did he experience personally from those things listed in verses 4 and 5 that made him best suited to make the claims he did?**

**Yet, from verse 10, they were always**

____________________ **and**

____________________ **everything.**

Tomorrow we will look at the "benefits" of suffering—those positive things suffering can produce. But beforehand, test your heart's standing by considering these probing questions.

- Could the suffering you experience be used as preparation for an intended purpose?
- Might you regard your trials as blessing, rather than crown it life's curse?

Consider that they just might be the crucibles in God's hands creating the masterpiece of Ephesians 2:10.

Day 2

# Product of Suffering

After a series of near-misses and mishaps, I told my dear friend, "The good Lord keeps saving me!"

With her usual depth of spiritual insight, she replied, "The Lord shields and protects us every day from all kinds of things we never see…some days it's just more obvious than others!"

How true that is!

I am overwhelmed when I think of the number of times and ways God has rescued me in dire straits. As I marveled in gratitude after this last experience, God brought me to the realization that if He never did one more thing for me, I would still be ultimately blessed beyond measure by the grace of His salvation.

## The Potential for Good

This is not a new revelation, for Paul frequently gave thanks and praise for his tribulations. In the midst of his suffering, he could be found rejoicing… because suffering has great potential.

**Read 2 Corinthians 1:8-11.**

**Check the boxes below that describe the outcome(s) of these tribulations from verses 9-11:**

- ☐ **They relied on God**
- ☐ **Had hope for deliverance**
- ☐ **Were helped by prayers of others**
- ☐ **Gave thanks for God's gracious favor**
- ☐ **Realized answered prayer**

I can't honestly say that I like the sound of the suffering part, but the outcome sounds great. Don't most of us want to realize those things that resulted from their suffering?

**Look at the situation you're "in." Pray to see it as God sees it, so that you may discern how or why He may be using it to prepare you.**

**Read 2 Corinthians 4:7-9. What was shown through these "jars of clay"?**

________________________________________________

**What adjective did he use to describe the power from**

**God?** ______________________________

**According to 2 Timothy 1:8, how did Paul tell Timothy he was able to suffer for the gospel?**

________________________________________________

**Have you experienced a time when you would not have come to know the power of God to get you through a situation unless you had to live through it? Explain.**

________________________________________________

________________________________________________

________________________________________________

But those experiences are not meant for us alone. They are meant to be shared.

"strengthening the disciples and encouraging them to remain true to the faith. 'We must go through many hardships to enter the kingdom of God,' they said." (*Acts 14:22*)

**Read Acts 14:21-22.**

**From verse 22 in the sidebar, consider the following:**

**Through what do we enter the kingdom of God?**

________________________________________________

**What did Paul and Barnabas do for other disciples?**

________________________________________________

**Write down what they said to them.**

______________________________________________

______________________________________________

**How might this help you?**______________________

______________________________________________

"I don't understand all the reasons we suffer for the Name. But I'm convinced of this: it is part of God's sovereign plan to prepare us to be His instruments of grace to a harsh and desperate world."

~ *Charles Swindoll (Paul: A Man of Grace and Grit)*

Paul and Barnabas strengthened and encouraged the disciples regarding the hard truth of suffering. But they also comforted them...*with the same comfort they received from God* (2 Cor 1:4).

**What suffering saint can you comfort, strengthen, or encourage today?**

______________________________________________

We are blessed with other strong words of encouragement from Scripture regarding the positive effects of suffering (far too many to cover in one day). But let's look at a few more, so that you might remain "true to the faith."

**Read 1 Peter 1:6-7.**

**The Christians still had cause to rejoice even though they had to ______________________________ .**

**What was the ultimate good it accomplished in their faith (vs 7)?**

______________________________________________

**Read Romans 5:3-4.**

**What does suffering produce?**

______________________________________________

______________________________________________

**Finally, read 2 Timothy 4:16-18.**

**Check those things to which Paul testified with full confidence:**

- ☐ **The Lord stood at his side**
- ☐ **The Lord gave him strength**
- ☐ **The Lord delivered him**
- ☐ **The Lord would bring him home**

**Are you able to make any conclusions from the suffering you have experienced?**

Not to reduce the gravity of suffering, for it can be catastrophic, crushing, and cruel, but can you agree with C. H. Spurgeon: "All our infirmities, whatever they are, are just opportunities for God to display His gracious work in us"?

## Day 3
# Prepared in Weakness

Now that he's 17 and a senior in high school, I know my son's days at home are becoming painfully fewer.

So, imagine my delight when he came to me, saying, "Mom, can we do a project together?"

He had come across a video on the Internet on how to make a homemade bow (as in a bow and arrow).

The bow is made from PVC. Key to the outcome is in softening the plastic. It had to first be made weak to be able to work with it and achieve the desired, finished result. Once it's pliable and arched, you then cool it to hold the form.

It had to first be made weak before it could be made stronger to achieve the desired, finished result. As long as it was rigid, it could not be remade with a new purpose.

## Having a Weakness to Boast About

The grueling travel of one of the Lord's first missionaries must have left him wrung out. I'm sure there were many days Paul felt sapped and spent. He wasted no time in being the first to admit it, however, so that others could see the power and glory of God.

**According to 1 Corinthians 2:3, in what state was he when he came to them?**

____________________________________________

____________________________________________

The Lord's servant entered Corinth by way of Athens. I encourage you to take the time to read of his experience there, from Acts 17:16-34. He weathered the pagan city alone, where debates and disputes arose with Jews, Greeks, Epicureans, and Stoics. Surrounded by their idols, he came up against great minds in philosophy and religion, only to gain few converts.

Oh, the list of human weaknesses (and I think I've known them all). Types include

- Physical
- Spiritual
- Personal
- Emotional
- Character
- Inabilities
- Unhealthy desires

For the most part, we will be discussing those spiritual and physical in nature. But always remember: El-Shaddai, our God Almighty, is able to help with them all.

"I will make them strong in the LORD, and they shall walk in His name, declares the LORD."

(*Zechariah 10:12, ESV*)

**Read 2 Corinthians 12:1-10.**

**Of what would he boast (vs 5)?**

___

**What is sufficient in weakness (vs 9)?**

___

**What did the Lord tell Paul about His power in weakness (vs 9)?**

___

**Finish the following statement: Paul was willing to boast all the more gladly about his weakness so that**

___

___

**Circle how Paul felt about his weakness from verse 10.**

**Frustrated**

**Discouraged**

**Content**

**Angry**

A "so that" statement in the Greek is referred to as a *hina* clause. A *hina* clause connects a biblical truth with its application and is used to describe a result—which is what we have in verse 9. Paul was happy to admit his weaknesses *so that* God's power would be manifest.

Weakness—in one form or another—is purely a facet of our human condition. And Paul didn't have any problem owning up to it, but for a specific purpose—the glory of God.

He "delighted in weakness"—his humanity and vulnerability—as opportunity..."for Christ's sake." He was content in mistreatment, trials, opposition, injustice, and adversity—all for the same reason...the *Only* reason.

**Why? Write the last sentence of verse 10.**

____________________________________________

____________________________________________

**Turn to Romans 8:26. Who helps us in our weakness?**

____________________________________________

**Read 1 Thessalonians 5:14.**

**What should we do for the weak?**

____________________________________________

**Match the verse to its powerful truth:**

| | |
|---|---|
| **1 Cor 2:3-4** | **We are strong in His power** |
| **2 Cor 12:9** | **Though weak, the Spirit's power was demonstrated** |
| **Eph 6:10** | **God's power is made perfect in weakness** |

Be encouraged, dear Christian. There is a direct correlation between our weakness and God's power.

I offer one more bit of encouragement from the pen of King David.

David's prayer in the face of a desperate predicament is recorded in Psalm 27. He gives excellent advice for the fainthearted.

**From Psalm 27:13-14 (NASB) below, underline what David did or commanded to do.**

**I would have despaired unless I had believed that I would see the goodness of the LORD in the land of the living. Wait for the LORD; be strong and let your heart take courage; yes, wait for the LORD.**

In your insufficiency, believe in God's goodness and grace. Trust in Him; rest in His power; and be infused with His strength.

Do not try to be strong in your own weakness. Trust and rest in Him, and He will be your strength.

In our weakness, should faith wane, the temptation to despair is a real threat. David would have, but didn't, because he believed. Believe, dear Christian. **When all else is weak, belief can still be strong.** So, when you're too weak to do anything, simply be still...and *believe*.

Allow faith to rise up and defeat the temptation to despair, lest doubt defeat you.

Believe in God's deliverance from this miserable moment. He can redeem the situation with the good that will come from it—because He is good.

Could it be that the resulting good is to be made better prepared?

And that bow? It **was** weak...but only for a time. It's strong as can be now. Strong enough to sling arrows far and wide.

Day 4

# Prepared in Seclusion

What a full week it has been already!

We ventured the crucibles Paul suffered for the sake of Christ and the advance of the gospel. And he taught us the good God brings from those trials.

Together, we examined the potential for positive outcomes of weakness and how wonderfully they shine a light on God's glory, power, and grace.

Now it's time to slow...and breathe. For here we settle in, to see how God prepares us in seclusion.

**Seclusion—** time set apart before the Lord, which He uses as periods of preparation. This practice proves particularly helpful in seasons of waiting.

## Becoming

Time alone with God is a necessary ingredient of our discipleship of Christ. Times of seclusion are not a time to grow more independent, but more dependent. Not to grow taller, but deeper. They don't have to be for long periods of time or in remote locations, but merely granting Him your undivided attention.

**Could it be that God wants to get you alone...still? What if He had your undivided attention? What might He accomplish if He had you all to Himself? Journal your thoughts here.**

Often God prepares first, before He equips and uses His saints as servants. And sometimes He must remove obstacles that cause distraction. There are numerous accounts of just such a practice.

**Match the person to his experience:**

| | |
|---|---|
| **Jacob** | **Two long years in prison (Gn 40:23-41:1)** |
| **Joseph** | **Shepherding 40 years in Midian (Acts 29:30)** |
| **Moses** | **Exiled to the isle of Patmos (Rev 1:9)** |
| **Elijah** | **A night with God in Bethel (Gn 28:15-16, 19)** |

**Paul's Timeline in Preparation of His First Mission Trip:**

- Conversion and Baptism in Damascus 34-36 AD
- Stay in Arabia 3 years
- Travel to Damascus and Jerusalem Several months
- Stay in Tarsus 6 missing years
- Stay in Antioch 1 year
- First Journey 44-46 AD (at approx. age 40)

*Dates are approximate and may vary*

| | |
|---|---|
| **Jesus** | **Hidden in God at the Kerith (1 Kg 17:2-5)** |
| **John** | **40 days in the wilderness (Mt 4:1-2)** |

There is no doubt that God grows and transforms us as He uses us—but only in connectedness to Him. However, there were times God removed His servants from an environment to prepare them for the next phase of their spiritual journey.

Paul was no exception.

**Read Galatians 1:17-21.**

**Where did God lead Paul after his Damascus Road conversion (vs 17)?**

________________________________________

**How long was he there (vs 18)?**

________________________________________

**What was his destination after leaving Jerusalem this time?** ________________________________

Paul headed for Arabia after his baptism. After three years he took a trip to Jerusalem for a brief visit with Peter and James and then traveled to Tarsus, where he remained for a period of approximately four to six years.

Paul states emphatically that what he learned, he received directly by revelation from Jesus Christ (see Galatians 1:12). Could it have been during these times removed?

Prior to his missionary career, Paul spent as much as ten years re-learning all he thought he knew of Holy Scripture. Then, when you factor in the amount of time he spent imprisoned (likely as much as five years), you get a real sense of just how much time he had alone with God.

There were even times he experienced abandonment.

**Read 2 Timothy 4:16-18 and fill in the blanks.**

**"But ___________________________________**

**___________________ and gave me strength."**

Through all of his experiences, Paul was becoming what God intended, so that he was able to declare, "I became a servant of this gospel by the gift of God's grace given me through the working of his power" (Eph 3:7).

**Read Mark 6:31-32.**

**What is the Lord's invitation extended to His disciples in these verses?**

_________________________________________________

"Very early in the morning, while it was still dark, Jesus got up, left the house and went off to a solitary place, where He prayed."

(*Mk 1:35*)

**How often do you accept His beckoning to go away to a quiet place with Him?**

_________________________________________________

On a more personal note, I would like to share how God prepared me for this study by interrupting my life. (Hardly on the scale of any real significance, but effective just the same.) There were two events that occurred back-to-back at the early stages of developing the idea for this study. They provided occasion for me to have secluded time with God to do nothing but pray and study. One evening I was involved in a car accident that sidelined me for six days. Immediately after that, there was a minor fire in our home. Everything stopped. All my busyness. All my plans. There was just He and I. I slowed to breathe and simply dwell in His presence. And I drank deeply from the well of His Word. It was a sacred time like no other. A time I could literally feel like He was preparing me to pen this work—for much was formulated, contemplated, and outlined during those stilled and quiet days. All the while, He was helping me become better prepared to begin this project you now hold in your hands.

For those in Christ, it's all a matter of becoming, you see.

God uses every facet of your life to *transform* your life. Each experience is an ingredient for your becoming—becoming more a reflection of Him.

# Prepared in Battle

Where our hearts stilled, pondering tranquil time alone with God yesterday, today they will *race* at the prospect of battle.

## Training Manual Required

The training manual entitled FM 7-1 "is the Army's doctrinal foundation for how to train."

(*militaryfieldmanuals.net*) (*mfm*)

"Training and instruction manuals are the nuts and bolts of every soldier's life."

(*naval-military-press.com*)

The best soldiers will tell you that to be prepared for battle, one must first know his training manual.

Let's see what *our* Manual says, soldier.

**Read 1 Samuel 4:1-11.**

**Who went to battle (vs 1)?**

____________________________________________

**After their first defeat, what did they decide to take into battle with them (vs 4)?**

____________________________________________

**Who was with the ark (vs 4)?**

____________________________________________

**What was the result?** ____________________

The first lesson we learn comes from the error the Israelites made in battle: They depended on something other than God for victory.

**Read Judges 3:7-11.**

**How did Othniel win this battle?**

____________________________________________

The second lesson teaches that power from the Spirit of the Lord is available to those obedient to God.

**According to Jeremiah 46:3, did the people need to prepare before they marched out to battle?** ___________

**What is the Lord called in Deuteronomy 33:29?**

_______________________________________________

"The horse is made ready for the day of battle, but victory rests with the LORD." (*Prv 21:31*)

**Read Psalm 44:1-3.**

**Paraphrase the history of God's people regarding battle.**

_______________________________________________

_______________________________________________

_______________________________________________

**Write Psalm 108:13:** ______________________________

_______________________________________________

_______________________________________________

So what's the third lesson? We are prepared **in** battle because God prepares us **for** battle. Thankfully, victory isn't dependent upon us, because God is our Shield and Defender.

**Read Ephesians 6:10-18.**

**What is commanded in verse 11?**

_______________________________________________

**With whom do we wrestle (vs 12)?**

_______________________________________________

_______________________________________________

Even being bound to a Roman guard prepared Paul in his work for the Lord. For in his chains he found opportunity to study their armor, thus lending visual aid for him to use in his letter to Ephesus.

**Complete the statement from verse 13:**

**"Put on the ___________ armor of God."**

**What are the darts Satan flings at you? (Fear, despair, discouragement, vanity?)**

______________________________________________

______________________________________________

**With what lies does he tempt you?**

______________________________________________

______________________________________________

There are two different Greek verbs used for "stand" in verse 13. The first one is *antistē nai* (*Thayers Greek Lexicon*). It means to withstand, to oppose or resist. The second command "to stand" at the end of the verse is *stē nai* (*Thayers Greek Lexicon*). It means "to make to stand; to stand ready or prepared." We must do both: resist and stand ready.

Victory results **only** in obedience—obedience to the Lord's commands and obedience to stand, shielded by the armor of God. We are commanded to wear essential battle armor so that we are prepared for inevitable and ongoing battle.

Did you notice something? There is no armor on the back. Ours is a forward advance only... *because God's got your back*!

To be prepared for battle, you must possess a training manual. Study more about our spiritual battle from our manual, the Bible. It has much to say in this regard so that we're always ready...and on guard.

**Prepared to Say**

"My grace is sufficient for you, for my power is made perfect in weakness. Therefore I will boast all the more gladly about my weaknesses, so that Christ's power may rest on me" (2 Cor 12:9).

*WEEK SIX*

# Prepared For

**DAY 1**

## What Lies Ahead

Now the exciting half of our study begins.

Now, we look ahead. Because, to be prepared **for** something, is to be prepared for what lies ahead.

If we aren't prepared for what lies ahead, the prospect can so fill us with paralyzing dread. Hopefully, this will alleviate that potential.

We have looked at how God prepared Paul. Now our focus shifts to what God prepared him **for**. It's the "why" he was prepared. We shift from circumstance to purpose—for there is purpose in all God does. And it applies to us—here and now—because we share with him some of those same things that matter most to God.

Though there may be purposes of God for our lives that we may never fully understand, there are some definite promises He has made for which we are to be prepared.

But we can't truly be prepared **for** anything until we are first in Christ.

"Remember the former things, those of long ago; I am God, and there is no other; I am God, and there is none like me. I make known the end from the beginning, from ancient times, what is still to come. I say, 'My purpose will stand, and I will do all that I please.'"

(*Isaiah 46:9-10*)

## A Coming to Prepare For

Echoing from eternity past is the word of the Lord to be prepared for His coming…first and final.

**How often do you think of the return of Jesus? Eternity?**

**How does the thought change your perspective? Values? Plans?**

**Does it make you anxious, fearful, or hopeful? Explain.**

**What does the life of one expecting the return of Jesus look like?**

**How does *your* life reflect that belief?**

**Read Matthew 25:1-13.**

"Be dressed ready for service and keep your lamps burning, like men waiting for their master to return from a wedding banquet, so that when he comes and knocks they can immediately open the door for him. It will be good for those servants whose master finds them ready, even if he comes in the middle of the night or toward daybreak. You also must be ready, because the Son of Man will come at an hour when you do not expect him."

(*Luke 12:35-36, 38, 40*)

**Summarize the parable:** ____________________

____________________

____________________

**What were the five bridesmaids with the oil called (vs 4)?**

____________________

**Circle the correct reason the maids were able to go into the banquet (vs 10):**

**Because they were rich**

**Because they were beautiful**

**Because they were ready**

**Because they were awake**

**Copy the valuable truth from Matthew 25:13.**

____________________

____________________

____________________

Jesus repeatedly stated that His disciples are to watch for His return. *How* to watch for His return? Be prepared! And how are we to be prepared for His appearing?

**Read Titus 2:11-14.**

**Circle the five definitives:**

**Do nothing but wait**

**Say "No!" to ungodliness**

**Live self-controlled lives**

**Live upright and godly**

**Be eager to do good**

**Live godly in today's world**

**Write Titus 2:13:** ________________________________

________________________________________

________________________________________

**Do you? In your waiting, do you have a "blessed hope"?**

**Read Psalm 63:1.**

**Do you share in David's same longing?**

**Read 1 Thessalonians 5:1-11.**

**Fill in the blanks from verse 4.**

**We are not in** ____________**so this day should not**

________________**us.**

**Since "we belong to the day," what are we to put on, according to verse 8?**

**1.** ________________________________

**2.** ________________________________

**3.** ________________________________

As the armor God provides for our battle (Ephesians 6:10-18), so, too, has He provided armor for our wait. And an essential piece of that armor is blessed hope. To live prepared for His coming is to live with hope…*and to share this hope.*

In closing today, I pray the words of Jude, our Lord's brother. I pray you keep yourself "in God's love as you wait for the mercy of our Lord Jesus Christ, to bring you to eternal life" (Jude 21).

Then Job replied to the Lord: "I know that you can do all things; no purpose of yours can be thwarted."
(*Job 42:2*)

Day 2

# Prepared for Death

The only way to be prepared for death is to be prepared for what follows death.

Death is a biological necessity for us to be able to go on to be with our Lord and begin the new life promised in Jesus.

There may be real emotional anxiety at the thought of death. And death may hold physical pain, but for the Christian, there is a blessed hope to calm the soul. There is an overcoming, so that we are able to confidently say with Paul: "Where, O death, is your sting?" (1 Corinthians 15:55)

"Medievals, Puritans, and later, evangelicals thought and wrote much about the art of dying well, and urged that our way of life should in truth be a preparation for leaving this world behind."

*~J. I. Packer (Knowing Christianity)*

## Comfort in the Uncomfortable

Although death may not be the most comfortable topic to discuss, there is comfort to be found in what the Bible says about it.

**Read 1 Corinthians 15:50-58.**

**According to verse 52, what shall happen to the dead at the trumpet sound?**

______________________________________________

______________________________________________

**What will become of our mortal bodies (vs 53)?**

______________________________________________

**What is Paul's all-important "therefore" in verse 58?**

______________________________________________

______________________________________________

**Read 2 Corinthians 1:8-10.**

**From verse 9, what did Paul feel? But what did he believe about it?**

______________________________

**How does he speak of God's deliverance (vs 10)?**

______________________________

What Paul suffered only served to strengthen his trust in God in the face of death. He spoke to God's deliverance in every tense—past, present, and future.

**Read 2 Corinthians 5:1-11.**

*Skenon* is the Greek word translated as "tent." It refers to a person's physical body. "Even if a believer's earthly body is destroyed, there is the assurance of a 'dwelling place' from God."

(*Hebrew-Greek Key Word Study Bible*)

**What is God's assurance in verse 1?**

______________________________

**Who has prepared us (vs 5)?** ______________________________

**How?** ______________________________

**Verse 7 says how we are to walk:**

______________________________

**What is our aim (vs 9)?** ______________________________

**What truth does Paul teach in verse 10?**

______________________________

**Complete the "therefore" in verse 11 (some translations may use "since").**

______________________________

This life continues into eternity. Meanwhile, these mortal, earthly bodies groan in longing to be clothed in our heavenly dwelling. Knowing what awaits us, we walk by faith, aiming to please our Lord, fully aware of the judgment to come. **BUT**…

**Fill in the blank from John 3:18:**

**"Whoever believes in Him is not**

**____________________________________."**

Grace makes us ready to face judgment and enter heaven.

"Our soul is on its way to God. [We] must live a holy life in preparation for the holy presence of God in heaven.

"The radical biblical perspective is to see death not as the termination of life but as the gateway to life.

"If you want to live we must die. And we will be willing to die only when we see the glories of the life to which death leads."

~*John Stott*
*The Radical Disciple*

**Finally, read 1 Thessalonians 4:13-18.**

**With what good news are we to encourage others?**

________________________________________

________________________________________

**How has looking at death eased or changed your thoughts about it?**

________________________________________

________________________________________

**What if you viewed this life as preparation for eternity?**

________________________________________

________________________________________

In contemplating the reality of death, there comes a realization of the greater reality of life. And with that, a deeper joy and appreciation for this one, brief life. Live it as Jesus purposed—to the fullest. But let death not find you unprepared. For greater, truer peace comes in the knowledge of being ready.

Day 3

## Prepared for Mentoring

This life? This wild, wonky, wonderful life? It's meant to be shared. As the saying goes, "No man is an island..."

What we learn in the training lab of bumps and bruises, failures and foibles, sensation and success are prime opportunities and object lessons to be used to bless the life of another. It actually adds significance and meaning to it all.

All of the experiences, circumstances, and situations we endure can fertilize the soil of another's growing faith when used to show the handiwork of God through mentorship.

**Look up in a concordance the number of times "mentor/ mentoring" is used in the Bible. How many occurrences did you find?**________________

**Look up and list synonyms for mentoring.**

________________________________________

________________________________________

Mentoring was practiced in ancient Grecian times. The word comes from the character named in Homer's *Odyssey*. Every religion and practice seems to have some mentoring system. Necessary components are relationship and communication.

Though *mentoring* is not used in the Bible, it's modeled practically cover-to-cover. It was not only a practice of Jesus, but was the essence of His command to "make disciples."

**What qualities do you believe are necessary for a Christian mentor?**

________________________________________

________________________________________

________________________________________

## The Nurturing Nature of Mentorship

If I were to paint a picture to depict my personal experience of being mentored by a dear sister-in–Christ, it would be of a hen gathering this chick under wings of grace—to guide, instruct, and model a life. And it is just that nurturing nature that epitomizes mentoring.

I've known many mentors in this walk, but the one primarily gifted by God has been one Debbie Weaver. (*I can practically hear her clucking denials at the mention.*) The goodness of God manifested to me has been the gift of her mentoring role in my life. And it has been one of such blessing that it works in me the desire to pass that blessing on as mentor to another daughter of His.

**Who has mentored you (either at school, in the workplace, in church, or as wife or mother)?**

________________________________________

This is precisely the biblical model portrayed for us. And there are no better examples than those in the life of Paul.

**From Acts 9:27 and Acts 11:25-26, who do you believe to be Paul's mentor?**

________________________________________

**Read Acts 18:1-4.**

**Who does Paul mentor, in turn?**

________________________________________

We further read in Acts 18 that Paul "spent some time in Corinth." It turns out that he was there for a year and a half (another component of mentoring: time). He then set sail for Syria, in the company of Priscilla and Aquila (Acts 18:18).

**Read Acts 18:24-26.**

**Who does Priscilla and Aquila then mentor in Ephesus?**

________________________________________

So we see the pay-it-forwardness of mentoring. We are mentored to mentor. God prepares us through mentors…for mentoring.

Let's learn more about what that looks like.

**What picture does Paul paint in 1 Thessalonians 2:7?**

______________________________________________

**Fill in the blanks from 1 Thessalonians 2:8 to get a better picture of what mentoring looks like:**

**Paul __________ for them, because he ___________ them, so he shared the ____________ and his ____________ with them.**

"I believe that mentoring is one of the most important strategies for growing the church into the next generation."

*~Bill Brewer as quoted in Christianity Today's article: "Good Mentoring"*

**How does he view his "brothers and sisters" ( see 1 Thes 2:1) in Thessalonica, according to 1 Thessalonians 2:20?**

______________________________________________

**How does Paul address Timothy in 1 Timothy 1:2?**

______________________________________________

**What is Paul's instruction to Timothy from 1 Timothy 4:12?** ______________________________________________

**Check the ways he was to "set an example":**

- ☐ **Speech**
- ☐ **Conduct**
- ☐ **Love**
- ☐ **Faith**
- ☐ **Purity**

Paul has much to teach us about mentoring—both in instruction and by example. In his instructions to the Philippians, Paul made a comment that I believe sums up the essence of the mentoree's role in mentorship, when he said, "Join together in following my example, brothers and sisters, and just as you have us as a model, keep your eyes on those who live as we do" (Php 3:17). But the key to what made his example so worthy of following is found in the comment he made to the Corinthians

**Write 1 Corinthians 11:1.**

______________________________

______________________________

______________________________

Paul also mentored Titus, another "true son in the faith" (Tit 1:4). He taught him the necessity to teach sound doctrine (Tit 2:1). But there was an expectation. They were to then teach and train those younger (see Tit 2:2-5).

**Read Titus 2:1-2.**

**Do you view mentoring, training younger men and women, as a command?** ______________

Titus was a Gentile preacher on the isle of Crete. The letter Paul wrote to him was penned within the last five years of his life.

**How is the woman mentor to live?**
**Circle all that are mentioned in Titus 2:3.**

**Reverent**

**Slanderous**

**Drunken**

**Teach what is good**

**According to Titus 2:4, what priorities are they to emphasize?**

______________________________

______________________________

There is no doubt about it: We are prepared for mentoring! And the Bible goes into great detail about what that is to look like.

Jesus was Paul's example. Paul learned to follow His example and taught others to do the same so that they could then be that example in training others.

It is mentioned twice in the Book of Acts that Paul went about "strengthening the disciples" (Acts 14:22; 18:23). I liken that to the Old Testament saying: "Build up, build up, prepare the road! Remove the obstacles out of the way of my people" (Is 57:14).

One way of doing just that is through mentoring.

Day 4

## What Paul Was Purposed For

I can't think of a more obvious example of someone being groomed for a certain position than a prince being groomed for kingship. Over the course of his life, he is trained and prepared for that end.

Each of us is purposed for something. The writer of Ecclesiastes identified "the whole duty of man" this way: "To fear God and keep His commandments" (Ecc 12:13). The variable is in how we live that out.

"No man can be making much of his life who has not a very definite conception of what he is living for."

*~Henry Drummond (The Radical Disciple)*

**Match three purposes stated in the New Testament with its verse.**

| | |
|---|---|
| **Conform to Christ** | **Mt 28:19** |
| **Make disciples** | **2 Cor 3:18** |
| **Reflect Christ** | **Rm 8:29** |

## Purpose Discovered

Some people know early on what they are meant to do. Paul thought he did. He was raised up and groomed to become a Pharisee of Pharisees.

Until Jesus took hold of him (Php 3:12), that is.

Through the direction of the Holy Spirit, Paul discovered what God had been preparing him for.

**Place a check mark in the column stating a role Paul was prepared for with regard to each verse listed. Note: all of the verses state multiple purposes.**

| Bible Verse | Apostleship | Preaching | Teaching | Serving | Evangelizing | Mentoring |
|---|---|---|---|---|---|---|
| Acts 20:17-20 | | | | | | |
| Rm 1:1 | | | | | | |
| Rm 1:9-10 | | | | | | |
| Gal 1:1 | | | | | | |
| Eph 3:7-8 | | | | | | |
| 1 Tm 2:7 | | | | | | |

Paul was all those things: an apostle, servant, teacher, preacher, evangelist, and mentor—those are the roles for which God had prepared him. All he endured and experienced in his upbringing, situations, trials, and suffering had purpose. And Jesus helped him to discover that purpose.

**According to Acts 13:47, with whom was Paul specifically supposed to share the gospel?**

______________________________________________

**In Acts 9:15-16 we read of the assignment Paul received to speak to Gentiles and ___________________________.**

We learn of Paul's missionary assignment when he addressed the crowd in the Jerusalem Discourse at his arrest (see Acts 22, esp. vs 21).

**Paul often referred to himself as a servant. State the two ways he became a servant of the gospel, as given in Ephesians 3:8.**

**1).** ____________________________________________

**2).** ____________________________________________

**From Ephesians 6:7-8, how are we commanded to serve?**

______________________________________________

**Paul's most earnest desire was to "gain Christ" (Php 3:8). What do you understand that to mean?**

______________________________________________

______________________________________________

______________________________________________

**Read Philippians 3:12.**

**Did Paul ever fully obtain his goal?** ______

**But, once he discovered what it was, how did he go after it?**

______________________________________________

"Paul, a servant of Christ Jesus, called to be an apostle and set apart for the gospel of God" (*Rm 1:1*).

With authority from God, an apostle had the right to speak as His delegate.

In conducting a translation comparison of Philippians 3:12, I noticed that some use the term "take hold" while others use the phrase "make it my own." According to the *Hebrew-Greek Key Word Study Bible*, the definition of the original Greek word is "to take eagerly; seize; possess; make one's own." It further states, "In allusion to public games: to obtain the prize with the idea of eager and strenuous exertion." Paul understood he was purposed to know and share Christ Jesus. Jesus called, prepared, equipped, and sent Paul on mission. And once he discovered what it was he was meant to do, he did it with all his might...all his days.

**Circle the purpose for which Paul called the Gentiles, as stated in Romans 1:5:**

**Obedience to their own will**

**Obedience that comes by faith**

**Conform to the world's example**

**Change the "you" pronoun in Romans 1:6 below to "I" and "are" to "am." Then reread the statement.**

**"And *you* also *are* among those called to belong to Jesus Christ."**

Jesus has called all of us *out* of the world. We are His. And He has sent us *into* the world...with purpose.

**Deeply consider 2 Timothy 1:8-9 (below).**

**How can you personalize this Scripture?**

**"So do not be ashamed of the testimony about our Lord or of me his prisoner. Rather join with me in suffering for the gospel, by the power of God. He has saved us and called us to a holy life—not because of anything we have done but because of his own purpose and grace. This grace was given us in Christ Jesus before the beginning of time."**

Day 5

# Works ~ It's What We're Prepared For

Yesterday we saw what Paul was meant to be (an apostle, evangelist and missionary) and what he was meant to do (to teach, preach and mentor). It is what he was prepared for.

God has not only prepared works of service for us (collectively and individually), but He has prepared us for those works.

Today is but an introduction into this topic of study, which will carry over through next week. When it comes to works, there is much to learn.

## Making Ready

John, the Baptist, as a type of Elijah, was prophesied to "make ready a people prepared for the Lord" (Mal 4:5-6).

Is that not a work for us all? Has not the Lord commanded the same of us, His disciples?

**Read from Luke 1:17 how John was to go about readying a people and circle those same methods that apply today:**

"Make ready for the Lord a people prepared."
(*Lk 1:17b ESV*)

**In the Spirit**

**Turn hearts**

**Turn the disobedient to wisdom**

**Make ready**

**Read Ephesians 4:11-13.**

**Circle why Jesus gave those leaders mentioned (vs 12):**

**To equip**

**To entertain**

**To ignore**

**They are to equip whom?**

______________________________

**They are to equip His people for**

______________________________

**They are to equip His people for works of service so that the Body may be built up until:**

______________________________

______________________________

Jesus was baptized and then readied for His public ministry of proclaiming the kingdom of God. He stated the work God sent Him to do when He quoted Isaiah 61:1 and the gospels further emphasize that work.

His work was undoubtedly unique. Though ours will not look the same, much of it is shared. And it will look different in the lives of each individual follower because we are each prepared differently to do a different work.

"Now in a great house there are not only vessels of gold and silver but also of wood and clay, some for honorable use, some for dishonorable. Therefore, if anyone cleanses himself from what is dishonorable, he will be a vessel for honorable use, set apart as holy, useful to the master of the house, ready for every good work."
*(2 Tm 2:20-21, ESV)*

**Read 2 Timothy 2:20-21 from the English Standard Version in the sidebar.**

**What does a "dishonorable vessel" need to do?**

______________________________

**Once cleansed, it is "holy, ____________to the master of the house.**

**For what is it ready? ______________________________**

**What promise is given in 2 Corinthians 9:8?**

______________________________

______________________________

**What is the good work (see verse 7)?**

______________________________

**Write Galatians 6:10:**

______________________________________________

______________________________________________

______________________________________________

At every opportunity we are to do good to all people—especially to those within the family of God. And we do that by being obedient to the work God has prepared for us.

In looking at what God has prepared us for, we come to realize why He has prepared this masterpiece; specifically, to do good works in "making ready for the Lord a people prepared."

May we all continue to serve until we all attain to the unity of faith, to the measure of the fullness of Christ Jesus, our Lord.

And may it be with the same attitude as Paul, so that we, too, are prepared to say....

**Prepared to Say**

"For to me, to live is Christ and to die is gain" (Php 1:21).

*WEEK SEVEN*

# The Works

## DAY 1
## Works in General

From eternity past God prepared a path for Jesus, the work of salvation. He walked that path in perfect obedience, bringing unequaled glory to God. And on His way to the cross, He completed various works.

We **are** a work
—God's work—
**to do** a work
—God's work.

The work prepared in advance for Paul could be viewed as the path he was to take. And he was obedient to do the work of the Lord in teaching and preaching along that path of apostleship.

The path God prepared for Paul and the works God did through him along that path were used in perfecting Paul, the masterpiece.

**From Acts 13:2 below, circle Who was speaking.**

**"While they were worshiping the Lord and fasting, the Holy Spirit said, 'Set apart for me Barnabas and Saul for the work to which I have called them.'"**

Upon returning to Antioch after their first missionary journey, we read in Acts 14:26 that Paul's team was "committed to the grace of God for the work they had now completed."

**To what were they handed over to complete the work?**

________________________________________

**Of what can you say is now a completed work for the Lord?** ____________________________________

The Holy Spirit issued the call and the grace of God helped them complete the work.

## What Can We Know About These Works?

When we dissected Ephesians 2:10 back in Week 2, we learned that God prepared good works in advance so that we would walk in them—as a path. Paul further instructs the saints in his epistles how to walk that path (or live our lives) in doing those works.

As God perfects us in working out our salvation, and as we discover our area of service and hone our skills and talents for the work He would have us do, this we can know for certain: There are works for us to do...and we are to do them. We are to be about our Father's business—because, after all, isn't God also, always working (Jn 5:17)?

What are we to be about doing? Jesus taught on the subject both in what He said and did. By His example in washing the disciples' feet, Jesus taught us to serve. In a statement recorded in Matthew 25, we learn of actions He found to be commendable and God-pleasing.

**Read Matthew 25:34-36.**

**What examples did Jesus give of acts that pleased the King?**

________________________________________

________________________________________

**Note an observation for each of the following verses:**

**Colossians 3:17** __________________________

**Colossians 3:23** __________________________

**Colossians 3:24** __________________________

Let's look again at a passage from Ephesians 4 from a slightly different angle.

**Read Ephesians 4:11-16.**

**How is it that the "whole body builds itself up in love"(vs 16)?**

________________________________________

There are some works spelled out in Scripture specifically for certain people. And then there are some works for us all. There are ways to serve those within the church and those outside the body of believers.

"Believers are God's workmanship in whom and through whom He performs good works."
(*The Bible Knowledge Commentary - New Testament*)

There are several options when it comes to works. But not doing them is not one of them. God has much for us to do.

There are works for many of us to do, yet those only **you** can do. There are some things that can only be done in your own unique way—as God has specifically prepared **you** to do them. They weren't meant for anybody else.

**Name something only you are meant to do:**

______________________________________________

Maybe this example will help explain: I have a dear friend from church with whom I work. Although we both work for the same company, we have different roles. She has a job to do, and I have a job to do. But there are some tasks we partner in to complete. We collaborate by using our own individual sets of skills, talents, and experiences. I can't do her part, and she can't do mine. But it takes both of us to get the whole job done.

God has given **all** of us works...and **each** of us works to do. We have to work together to do them...but separately.

The church as a whole is charged with clear responsibilities and we accomplish those works together, as one body. But we each have a contribution to make. It is imperative to do your part—the part only you can do. It may be the same as what someone else is doing...but it's entirely different—because you're the one doing it.

I urge you to find a mentor who will help you discover, develop, and mature in servanthood.

But be prepared for the unexpected.

**Read Philippians 1:12-14.**

**According to verse 12, what was the greater "work"?**

___________________________________________

**According to verse 14, what was accomplished?**

___________________________________________

**According to verse 13, what became clear to everyone?**

___________________________________________

**Complete this thought from verse 14:**

**Because of ___________, the people became confident in the Lord and fearlessly proclaimed the gospel.**

God still had work for Paul to do even though he was in chains. The work the Lord might have you do may not be what you expected or look like what you imagined, but that might be precisely what makes it effective. Even though Paul was in prison, he continued to do the work of the Lord—because a work can be done from wherever you may find yourself.

**What can be done from right where you are?**

# On Assignment

Man has got a job to do. An important job.

It has always been so.

Wasn't it King Solomon who said, "There is nothing new under the sun" (Ecc 1:9)?

God issued the first assignment in the Garden.

**Read Genesis 1:26-28 and 2:15 and note God's assignment.**

____________________________________________

____________________________________________

Works—they're as old as creation. In the beginning God charged man to work the ground and govern the other creatures. Man was created with purpose. We were created to be God's image-bearers and to partner in relationship with Him to care for what He created.

**Much has changed since then. What does the assignment God issued to Adam look like in our modern world?**

____________________________________________

____________________________________________

And when He created the nation of Israel, He gave them assignments as well.

"Then the LORD said: 'I am making a covenant with you. Before all your people I will do wonders never before done in any nation in all the world. The people you live among will see how awesome is the work that I, the LORD, will do for you.'" (*Ex 34:10*)

## Work for One, Work for All

**God said He would do an awesome work (see Ex 34:10 in the sidebar). Read the four verses that follow, and match the verse with what they first had to do.**

**Vs 11** **Smash idols**

**Vs 12** **Worship God alone**

**Vs 13** **Make no agreements with the enemy**

**Vs 14** **Obey**

**Read Exodus 35:25-26.**

**All the women who had ___________________ and were ___________________ spun.**

**What are your skills?**

**Are you willing?**

**What are you willing to do for the Lord with the skill you have?**

**Read Exodus 35:29-36:1.**

**Who commanded the work (vs 29)?**

_______________________________________________

**Who was chosen (vs 30)?**

_______________________________________________

**He was able because (vs 31)**

_______________________________________________

**Were they all given the same job (vs 35)?**

**From Exodus 36:1 note what the work was:**

_______________________________________________

**Who did the work?** _______________________________

"The purpose of the gifted men is to prepare God's people for works of service. More literally, this purpose is for the perfecting or equipping of the saints unto the work of the ministry. Gifted people are to minister the Word to others so that they in turn are readied to get involved in ministering to others."

God prepared the people in their skill and provided the materials and the opportunity to do the work He had prepared for them to do.

There was plenty of work to go around. There was work for the Kohathites, Gershonites, Merarites, and the Levites, and all the other clans of Israel (see Numbers 4).

**What work does He have for your clan?**

There was the work prepared for **all** of them—building the tabernacle. And the work prepared for **each**—in using their individual trades for specific articles. Some worked on the curtain, some the tent, others the furnishings and utensils. Some worked with wood, some stone, and others gold. They pooled their skills and resources and went to work. And when the work was finished the glory of the Lord filled the tabernacle (Ex 40:33-35).

**Record your findings from Deuteronomy 2:7:**

____________________________________________

____________________________________________

In the desert place, the people were assigned work to do, but God blessed them to do it...even there.

Day 3

# The Order of Works

There is no denying the fact that Christianity has its own lingo. There are certain words and phrases coined "church words" because that is primarily where they were born and are predominantly used.

*Fruit* is one of them. When used, it often refers to a product, outcome, or result.

As cooking is something we do because God provides food (as illustration, we'll tag cooking as the fruit of provision), works are something we do as a fruit of salvation. Though we may not be able to determine which came first in the whole chicken-or-the-egg debate, we can know what came first in the works vs.grace debate—because works are born from God's gracious gift of our salvation.

**Read Titus 3:3-8.**

**Complete the sentence from verse 5:**

**He saved us because** ________________________________

**Is it because of anything we have done?**

**According to Jesus' own words quoted in Mark 10:18,**

**who is considered "good"?**________________________

Works are...

the evidence of faith
and
the fruit of salvation.

## The Why of Works

In our study today I will offer three answers to the "why" question of works.

**Read Ephesians 2:8-10.**

**We are saved** _____ ______________.

"Upon being caught in sin in the garden, rather than cry to God for mercy, he sewed fig leaves together to cover his nakedness. He relied on his works rather than God's grace."
*~Dick Hillis*
(DayBook of Promise)

**Is it given or earned?** ___________

**Which does Paul explicitly mention first, grace or works?**

___________________________________________

**We are the masterpiece, created in Christ Jesus to**

_____________________________.

We are created in Him first (because He *first* loved us [1 John 4:19]) to then bear the fruit of good works.

It is imperative that we get the proper order of works aligned in our minds so as to keep our motives pure and our spirits rightfully humble.

But notice, in reading Ephesians 2:8-10, that several elements are directly connected. As saving grace is connected to faith, works are connected to the gift. And all are connected to the One through Whom salvation was wrought, Jesus Christ.

This passage not only defines for us the proper order of salvation and works, it clearly answers our first "why" of works: because we are saved. It is the fruit of salvation.

We are saved not *by* good works but *for* good works.

**Why do *you* do "good works"?**

___________________________________________

___________________________________________

___________________________________________

Good works flow from the love and gratitude of what Jesus has done for us.

The answer to our second "why" about works is found in James's epistle.

**Read James 2:14-18.**

**Why do we do good deeds or works?**

___________________________________________

Our deeds are evidence of true faith. And true faith naturally expresses itself in meeting the needs of others.

These works don't have to be a grand feat. You don't have to organize a spectacular event. It doesn't even have to be religious in nature. It doesn't have to be extraordinary, but rather it is often exemplified in the ordinary things in meeting another's needs, like raising a family or caring for elderly parents. It's not necessarily *what* we do but *how* we do it (lovingly in His name and humbly by His power). And *why* we do it.

**What would you classify as good works?**

______________________________________________

______________________________________________

______________________________________________

Essentially, we are to love God and love others. Wouldn't those things we do out of love for Him and in meeting the needs of others be considered a good work?

**Can all we commit to God as an offering, done by His grace, be considered good works?**

______________________________________________

In every season of life, all of life can amount to a good work when committed and offered to God. For from the knowledge that we are loved flows a "devotion to do good works" (Titus 3:8), so that others may also gain that same knowledge of God's love.

Jesus best summed up our "why" of good works, which brings us to our third reason in today's session.

**Write that reason from the statement recorded in Matthew 5:14-16:**

______________________________________________

Though works are the fruit of salvation, God's glory is, hopefully, the goal and the fruit of our works.

**What are our three "whys for works"?**

**1)** ______________________________________

**2)** ______________________________________

**3)** ______________________________________

The works we do are not works to earn favor. Our works are not to earn salvation (before-the-fact) or done as a payment owed for our salvation (after-the-fact). Rather, they are done in faith, obedience, and love as a response to God. We do them not to be saved, or because we have been saved, but to glorify God as an expression of faith and the worship and gratitude that rises from our salvation.

**Do you have a sense of the work God has prepared for you? Explain.**

____________________________________________

____________________________________________

**Do you have a sense of preparedness that you are prepared for the works God would have you do? Explain.**

____________________________________________

____________________________________________

## Day 4
# More Working Questions Answered

When I want answers to the questions that plague me, I am persistent with my questions. Works are no exception. We've been asking "working" questions all week. We found ourselves on Day One asking the "what" question of works. On Day Three we asked the "why" of works. Here, on Day Four, we will seek to understand the "how" of works.

We've determined what works are and the acceptable motives for them. We haven't, however, sought out all there is to learn on the matter. So we'll keep asking so that we may gain a better understanding of the proper attitudes of works.

## The How of Works

The Thessalonians modeled work for us. In studying Paul's commendation of their labor, both our "how" and "why" questions are answered.

**Read 1 Thessalonians 1:3, and take note of what you learn from their example.**

_______________________________________________

_______________________________________________

_______________________________________________

Their works were produced by faith and prompted by love (foundational in our labor for Christ, as we discovered last week). Faith, hope, and love are the best motives **and** attitudes for every deed done.

**Peter also wrote about how we are to serve. Circle the phrases that complete 1 Peter 4:11:**

**Whoever serves is to serve**
**By his own strength**
**With plenty of help**
**By God's strength**
**As best he can**

**So that**
**In everything**
**Sometimes**
**In some things**
**Once in awhile**
**God may be glorified**
**Through the church**
**Through His people**
**Through ministers**
**Through Jesus Christ**

**To Him belong glory and power forever and ever.**

______________________________________________

**What similarities do you notice in statements made by Jesus and Paul about how they labored for God?**

**Compare and note your findings from John 14:10 and Colossians 1:29:**

______________________________________________

______________________________________________

Paul knew his competence came from God (2 Cor 3:5), for He alone is able.

**How able? (See Ephesians 3:20-21)**

______________________________________________

We must not forget that the works done for the Lord in the advance of the gospel are not always pleasant or easy. There are times when more is required of us than rocking babies in the nursery or cooking a dish for a Sunday church potluck.

**To what extent did Epaphroditus serve the Lord, as found in Philippians 2:30?**

________________________________________

Epaphroditus and Paul, along with the other apostles and multitudes of the Lord's servants since, willingly risked their lives for the sake of Christ.

**In the face of adversity, how was Paul able to do the Lord's work noted in 2 Timothy 4:17?**

________________________________________

Paul pretty much answers all the questions we could have about how we are to serve the Lord by our works. So we will close today with three key verses of his on the matter.

**What does Paul tell us in Ephesians 3:7 about how he became a servant of the gospel?**

________________________________________

**What should our working attitude be according to Philippians 2:14?**

________________________________________

**How should our deeds be done, as noted by Paul in Colossians 3:17?**

________________________________________

God "is watching the way you handle the little jobs. If you are faithful with a few matters, He will set you over many (Mt. 25:21). The reward of good work is greater work. Do you aspire to great things? Excel in the small things. Show up on time. Finish your work early. Don't complain."

*~Max Lucado*
(*You'll Get Through This*)

Day 5

## The Only Way to Work

Their senior year was a barrage of questions. Well, actually, just one nagging question. Practically everyone my kids encountered had the same question playing on repeat for them: "So, what do you want to be?"

It was too early in their lives to know for certain what career path to take, let alone what they wanted to do with the rest of their lives. They were still discovering their abilities, interests, passions, skills, and gifts. They had not yet experienced enough of life to be able to answer such a big question.

"If I am to go on living in the body, this will mean fruitful labor for me."

~ *The Apostle Paul,* (*Philippians 1:22*)

**When did you know?**

**Did you ever change your mind?**

Though they may not know specifically how they will live out their future, they can know how to live out their days in the process of figuring that out—we all can. There can be knowing in not knowing because we can still know "right" even if we don't know "what."

Maybe you haven't quite figured it all out yet either, but there are things we can know when it comes to how to live lives of faith that are pleasing to God.

And you may not know what "work" it is that He would have you do in serving the Body of Christ, but there are some things we can know to do. And the one main thing to do before, during, and after is to pray!

**Decisions, decisions! What factors do you consider in making decisions about the areas and ways to serve?**

**How do you go about making those decisions?**

# In the Best of Times, in the Worst of Times; All the Time: Pray

The absolute best work EVER...always...is prayer.

It's not only a "work" to do, it is the only way to do any work.

The Bible clearly teaches that we have all been given different gifts of God's grace (Rm 12:6) so that we may bring Him glory in serving and blessing others. We must evaluate where those gifts lie and how to employ them for the benefit of the body.

**For what "gifts of the Spirit" does 1 Corinthians 14:12 tell us we should be eager?**

________________________________________

**Circle what we should do with those gifts:**

**Ignore them**

**Excel in them**

**Diminish them**

**What do you learn about how to use our gifts in 1 Peter 4:10?**

________________________________________

The gifts God has given us are not for our own fulfillment, while we can enjoy great satisfaction in using them, but rather to be used responsibly in service to Him and others.

Maybe you're unsure of where or how to serve. Maybe you haven't quite figured out your strengths and gifts. And maybe you don't feel prepared. Then, here is a prayer challenge for you. Pray these two verses every day for the next 30 days. Memorize them. Change the pronouns and pray it for yourself. And be sure to pray it for others, by name, as well as for your church. Then come back and see how God is working in answer to this prayer.

**"Now may the God of peace, who through the blood of the eternal covenant brought back from the dead our Lord Jesus, that great Shepherd of the sheep, equip you with everything good for doing His will, and may He work in us what is pleasing to Him, through Jesus Christ, to Whom be glory for ever and ever. Amen." (Heb 13:20-21)**

Commit to reflect prayerfully upon your gifts, talents, and interests and ask God to show you the work He has prepared for you to do. Once He shows you what that is, pray for equipping. And then pray all the while you work.

Pray always—it's the only way to work.

In closing today, I pray this prayer regarding our works:

**May these things be remembered before our God:**

**Your work produced by faith;**
**Your labor prompted by love;**
**And your endurance inspired by hope in our Lord Jesus Christ.**
**(1 Thess 1:3)**

We touched on several questions regarding works this week. We looked at the what, why, and how perspectives in answering some of those questions. One thing from Ephesians 2:10 we know for certain is that God has a work He prepared in advance for us all. Through study and prayer, may you realize what that work is so that you feel prepared to say with Paul:

**Prepared to Say**

"I thank Christ Jesus our Lord, who has given me strength, that He considered me trustworthy, appointing me to His service" (1 Tm 1:12).

WEEK EIGHT

# Prepared To

DAY 1

## Prepared To: Listen

Our time together is moving right along! I commend you for your dedication to the study of God's Word and for diligently working your way to this point.

We have covered a lot since learning what God uses to prepare us. We took time to discover how God prepares us through circumstances; how we are prepared by various agents; and then how God prepares us in our experiences. Week Six moved us to learn the purposes for which we are prepared, which then transitioned us to the works of Ephesians 2:10 that we are both prepared for and that God has prepared for us. Now we advance to how we are prepared to...prepared to act and respond according to the work God has done in us.

Besides works, what are we prepared to do? Well, you can't know what that is until you listen.

### Primed and Ready

I remember the winters from my youth in northern Michigan as being harsher than they really were. I may not have dementia...yet; but I'm sure my memories have the snow deeper and the temps far colder than they actually were.

However, I do remember vividly the monster of a fuel oil furnace we had. And I remember watching my dad lighting it when it went out. He always had to prime it with fuel oil to get it to ignite.

I also remember the old-fashioned hand water pump we used to get water from our well. It had the same sort of issue. If it ran dry, you had to prime it with water to get the flow going.

Listening is like that. You have to prime your hearing first by listening. You have to listen to hear. And the more you listen, the more you learn to hear.

**Circle the state of those who wouldn't listen to God as stated in Ezekiel 3:7.**

**"But the people of Israel are not willing to listen to you because they are not willing to listen to Me, for all the Israelites are hardened and obstinate."**

**Read Luke 18:22-23.**

**How did the rich young ruler respond to what Jesus had to tell him?** ____________________

"The gatekeeper opens the gate for him, and the sheep listen to his voice. He calls his own sheep by name and leads them out. "My sheep listen to my voice; I know them, and they follow me."

(*John 10:3, 27*)

Sometimes we are too proud or stubborn to listen. And sometimes Jesus says something hard...something we don't want to hear. Not in an audible voice, mind you, but in the leading and conviction of the Holy Spirit. In many areas, however, He has already spoken...through His Word.

**What has been something difficult for you to hear?**

____________________

There have been times when God's people have been prepared to listen for a message from Him. Sometimes it required waiting, as in Abraham's case. Samuel was prepared to listen when God told him to prepare the next king. Ananias listened when God told him to prepare His next missionary. And God prepared Cornelius to listen to an unexpected visitor from a foreign culture.

**Read Acts 10:1-7.**

**From verse 2, what were three things that prepared Cornelius to listen to God?**

**1)** ____________________

**2)** ____________________

**3)** ____________________

**Read Acts 10:17-23.**

**What was Peter told to do in verse 20?**

______________________________________________

**How did he prepare to listen (go back to verse 9)?**

______________________________________________

Their listening was key to the advance of the gospel to the Gentiles and the growth of the early church. But they would never have known how to respond to God had they not first been prepared to listen.

There is one thing we can know about listening: The more we listen, the more sensitive we will become to hear.

We can prepare to listen by praying the words of Samuel found in 1 Samuel 3:10:

"Speak, for your servant is listening."

Day 2

# Prepared To: Move On

"For we live by faith, not by sight."

(*2 Corinthians 5:7*)

The Greek word translated here as "live" is *peripatoumen*, which means walk. The short definition in Strong's Concordance is "conduct my life."

To live life is to live by faith.

To live by faith is to walk (according to 2 Corinthians 5:7) and to walk is to move on.

We Christians are definitely to move on, walking by faith. The work God does in preparing us is not to arrive at a certain point and then stay there. No! We are prepared to move on.

## What Keeps Us from Moving

Unfortunately, there are several obstacles that hinder our momentum for forward movement.

**What caused God to tell Samuel to move on in 1 Samuel 16:1?**

_______________________________________________

**What two things put obstacles in the Corinthian believers' way?**

**Paul's teaching**

**False teaching**

**Brothers and sisters**

**People causing division**

**What can be a hindrance that's mentioned in 2 Corinthians 2:10-11?**

_______________________________________________

Others can keep us from moving on, as can division, false teaching, and the unwillingness to forgive.

**Read Romans 6:1-4.**

We were buried with Christ in baptism and given a new life. Shall we go on living as before? No! He has set us on a new path to move on in a new direction.

**Read Galatians 5:24.**

Now given a new life and a new way to walk, we are to walk led by the Spirit.

**Read 1 Corinthians 9:24-25.**

Once prepared does not necessarily mean always prepared. In this race of faith, it takes continued training and self-control to keep running forward… toward our heavenly prize.

**Read Colossians 3:5-10.**

**According to verse 5, what can keep you from moving on?**

____________________________________________

**What must we get rid of (vs 8)?**

____________________________________________

____________________________________________

Sometimes energy wanes, zeal fades, boredom invades, and obstacles drain. We all have the potential to revert, slow down, or stall out. Our new self must be continually "renewed in knowledge in the image of its Creator."

"Continue to work out your salvation with fear and trembling." (*Philippians 2:12b*)

**What disciplines can you form to continually renew your mind with the gospel of grace?**

Paul kept moving on; each experience strengthened his faith and prepared him for God's next thing.

Move on, along the path God has prepared for us—living by faith, Christian.

In closing today, I want to share something with you that I came across in my studies. I pray it blesses you as much as it did me:

> "It is all prepared, and we only have to walk in it, with God, one step at a time. Put your hand into God's, look up into His face, saying, 'Lead me Father, in the prepared way. Teach me Thy way. Make me to know the way wherein I should walk.' What confidence is here! The only serious matter is to discover the prepared path."
>
> *F. B. Meyer*
> *(15 Key Studies from the Heart of Ephesians:*
> *A Topical Commentary)*
> *(Meyer)*

Day 3

# Prepared To: Grow

Part of our being prepared to listen and to move on is to grow because, having been made alive in Christ, that's what living things do; they grow. And they grow…and grow…and grow.

## Growing on to Maturity

Everything God uses to prepare us He can also use to grow us. And the more we grow spiritually—growing in our faith and trust in God—the more mature we become.

**Read Colossians 1:28-29.**

**To what did Paul toil and strive?**

____________________________________________________

**Who is to be presented fully mature (vs 28)?**

____________________________________________________

**Read Hebrews 6:1-2.**

**What is the expectation (vs 1)?**

____________________________________________________

**What longing promotes growth, according to 1 Peter 2:2 in the sidebar?**

____________________________________________________

"Like newborn babies, crave pure spiritual milk, so that by it you may grow up in your salvation."
(*1 Peter 2:2*)

**What do you equate with "spiritual milk"?**

____________________________________________________

There can be no growth apart from regular Bible study, for to have a steady diet of Scripture, is to be nourished. And nourishment always equals growth.

**Read 1 Corinthians 3:1-3.**

**What might be a sign of immaturity (vs 1)?**

______________________________________________

**For what did Paul commend his brothers and sisters in Christ in 2 Thessalonians 1:3?**

______________________________________________

Our life in Christ is a growing life. We are to grow on to spiritual maturity. And to live mature spiritually is to live a godly life. Quite simply, you cannot have spiritual maturity without godliness.

## Godliness

"Godliness is more than Christian character; it is Christian character that springs from a devotion to God…a devotion to God that results in a life that is pleasing to Him."

~*Jerry Bridges* (*The Practice of Godliness*)

A godly life is a life filled with God, built upon God, and centered around God. A godly life is a life devoted to pleasing God.

**How do you perceive growing and godliness linked, according to Paul's instruction in 1 Thessalonians 4:1?**

______________________________________________

______________________________________________

______________________________________________

**Read 1 Timothy 4:7-8.**

**What was the goal of training (vs 7)?**

______________________________________________

**What "has value for all things" (vs 8)?**

______________________________________________

**According to Titus 1:1, what leads to godliness?**

______________________________________________

**What kind of lives does Titus 2:11-13 tell us to live?**

______________________________________________

______________________________________________

The Bible contains a wealth of material on the subject of maturity and godliness. They absolutely must be included in any discussion about being prepared. However, trying to abbreviate these two critically significant topics into one day's study was extremely difficult. I hope you found the coverage sufficient in establishing their importance in the growing process of our spiritual lives in Christ. I also hope it has produced a desire to know more, moving you to further study; because study produces growth…
and to grow is to prepare.

May you "stand mature and fully assured in all the will of God."

(*Prayer adapted from Colossians 4:12b, ESV*)

Day 4

## Prepared To: Reflect Glory

I love photographs of a lakeside landscape when the surface of the water is so smooth that it perfectly reflects its surroundings. You hardly know where the water ends and the bank begins. In fact, the reflection is so clear, so pure, it almost creates an optical illusion, of sorts, and you can't quite tell one from the other. The sheer beauty of such a scene is nothing short of breathtaking.

Oh, to reflect the Lord's glory like that!

**If you were to take a picture of the landscape of your heart, how do you see your heart reflecting God's heart?**

___

___

___

We are prepared to grow and to move on to Christlikeness. And, like Christ, we are prepared to reflect God's glory.

This brings to mind something Max Lucado wrote, "God's to-do list consists of one item: 'Reveal my glory.'"

"But all of us who are Christians have no veils on our faces, but reflect like mirrors the glory of the Lord. We are transfigured by the Spirit of the Lord in everincreasing splendour into his own image."

(*2 Corinthians 3:18, Phillips*)

**Read Romans 15:8-9.**

**For what are we to glorify God?**

___

**What does Paul tell us we are to do for the glory of God, as found in 1 Corinthians 10:31?**

___

**How did Jesus say He brought God glory, as recorded in John 17:4?**

______________________________________________

## Christ-Reflectors

In *The Radical Disciple*, John Stott points out that "God wants His people to become like Christ, for Christlikeness is the will of God for the people of God (29)."

**How is Jesus described in Hebrews 1:3?**

______________________________________________

______________________________________________

**Write 1 John 2:6.**

______________________________________________

______________________________________________

**What is our instruction from Philippians 2:5 regarding relationships?**

______________________________________________

"The New Testament teaches that true spirituality comes about through gradual growth and changes brought about in us by the power of Christ. This is why no one of us has "arrived" spiritually; we are all seeking to walk with Christ more closely than ever before and to mold ourselves more nearly into His own likeness."

*~Rubel Shelly* (*Going on to Maturity*)

Just as the moon reflects the light of the sun, so are we to reflect the glory of God in all we do. That's easier said than done, however. But we are told this is the transforming work of the Holy Spirit—by Whom all things are possible. As we increasingly become more and more like Jesus, that is precisely what we will do.

In one of his letters to the Corinthians, Paul wrote about the change being done in us so that we may see and reflect the Lord's glory.

**Read 2 Corinthians 3:13-18.**

**What does "ever-increasing" mean to you?**

---

The Greek word translated as "transformed" in 2 Cor 3:18 is *metamorphóō*. Look familiar? It means "transformed after being with; transfigured."

*HELPS Word Studies* (*Bible Hub*)

The veil has been removed so that we may look upon the Lord's glory and by the Spirit of the Lord become more and more like Him—reflecting that glory in increasing measure.

In his letter to the Thessalonians, Paul penned a prayer that God would sanctify them "through and through" (1 Thes 5:23). Sanctification is the process of becoming more like Christ. It is a prayer within the will of God that bears repeating.

Think back to my opening illustration. Picture God drawing the masterpiece of you. He sketches the outline, but how you fill in the resemblance is up to you. And whether or not there is a reflection He has also left up to you. But a devoted heart, surrendered to the sanctifying will and work of the Master does become like Christ. And that likeness? Well, that is His Glory.

**How does the masterpiece He is creating in you reflect His glory?**

Day 5

# Prepared To: Hope

The silent thief came in the night, robbing spunk and freedom from sweet Ruthie.

Difficult days marched on as she struggled with the most common tasks of daily living. On a particularly good day, when she was more aware and alert, and her personality seemed temporarily in place, I knelt before her wheelchair and simply asked, "How you feelin,' Ruthie?"

"I'll just be glad when I'm free."

Such few words to convey her profound belief! Her frustration was both evident and understood. I was relieved to know that she clung to something far greater than that chair. Her hope had not been stolen that fateful night. Nor had her faith.

She awaited the day—a day for her emancipation—when her body would no longer fail her and hold her captive.

The only response I could choke past the joy: "He hears you, Ruthie. He hears the cry of your heart."

It would seem that hope is the first line of attack for our enemy, as if it were marked with a giant bullseye. Thankfully, it is often impenetrable and defiant.

## A Medley of Essential Verses on Hope

Hope—it watches. Or it is unready. If it doesn't watch, it misses the help of God when it comes...*and it always comes.*

**Psalm 62:5 names the Source of hope as:**

_______________________________________________

**First Timothy 1:1 tells us Who our hope is.**

_______________________________________________

"Hope in Scripture is the absolute certainty of a believers' victory in God."

~*The Bible Knowledge Commentary* (*Hoehner*)

**The basis of our hope is found in 1 Peter 1:3:**

______________________________________________

> "Hope is not dependent on peace in the land, justice in the world, and success in the business. Hope is willing to leave unanswered questions unanswered and unknown futures unknown. Hope makes you see God's guiding hand not only in the gentle and pleasant moments but also in the shadows of disappointment and darkness."
>
> ~*Henri Nouwen* (*Turn My Mourning Into Dancing*)

**Peter praises God in the same verse as the God Who, in His great mercy, has given us a new birth into:**

**A failing hope**

**A fading hope**

**A dying hope**

**A living hope**

**Titus 2:13 states the "blessed hope" we are waiting for:**

______________________________________________

**What was Paul's hope, mentioned in 2 Corinthians 1:9-10?**

______________________________________________

Our hope will never fail us because it is rooted in the God who will never fail us. It is built upon the sure foundation of what Jesus has already accomplished and the infallible promises of a sovereign and faithful God.

**Read Hebrews 6:19.**

**What is our hope called?**

______________________________________________

**How is it described?**

______________________________________________

Hope is an anchor when the storms of life batter faith. Peter calls it a "living hope" that sustains in suffering from trials that "prove the genuineness of faith" and results in the outcome of our faith, "the salvation of our souls" (1 Peter 1:7, 9).

**Fortify your hope by reading Hebrews 10:32-39.**

"Those who hope in Me will not be disappointed." (*Isaiah 49:23b*)

Ultimate hope confidently says, "Come, Lord Jesus!"

I will close today with a prayer for our hope from Ephesians 1:18-19:

> "I pray that the eyes of your heart may be enlightened in order that you may know the hope to which He has called you, the riches of His glorious inheritance in His holy people, and His incomparably great power for us who believe."

Through all the seasons and circumstances of this life, God continues to prepare us. He prepares us to listen, to move on, to grow, to reflect His glory, and to hope.

Are you prepared to boast with Paul "in the hope of the glory of God?

**Prepared to Say**

"Through Jesus we have gained access by faith into this grace in which we now stand. And we boast in the hope of the glory of God" (Rm 5:2).

*WEEK NINE*

# Walking Prepared

**DAY 1**

## Living the Walk

Just as there are different attitudes and behaviors, there are different ways to walk. You can stride, strut, parade, glide, trudge, limp or crawl. (Hopefully, not all in a given day!)

The Greek verb *peripateó*, often translated "walk," means: "to live; to regulate one's life; to conduct."

And if the way you walk spiritually is the way you live your life, then you can walk by virtue or vice, spirit or flesh.

As Christ followers, we are commanded to live a certain way, to walk in a certain manner.

Ephesians 4:17 declares, "Now this I say and testify in the Lord, that you must no longer walk as the Gentiles do, in the futility of their minds" (ESV).

**What are ways you can walk differently from the world?**

________________________________________

________________________________________

________________________________________

**From 1 Timothy 6:11-12, what does Paul say we are to do (vs 11)?**

________________________________________

________________________________________

**What does it mean to you to "pursue" something?**

________________________________________

**And we can! Because 2 Peter 1:3-4 says that God has**

**prepared us—He has ____________ ________________**

**______________________________________________**

> "Holiness is not a series of do's and don'ts, but conformity to the character of God and obedience to the will of God. Accepting with contentment whatever circumstances God allows for me is very much a part of a holy walk."
>
> ~*Jerry Bridges* (*Pursuit of Holiness*)

God has given us **everything** we need to walk with Him and pursue righteousness—that we may live a godly life and participate with Him in His divine nature.

To quote Paul: "Fight the good fight," dear friend; "take hold of eternal life" (1 Timothy 6:12).

## The Path

The path we are to walk is the path of holiness. We are to follow Jesus in obedience. He is our path. When we do, we walk in light and life (Jn 8:12).

**Match to complete:**

| | | |
|---|---|---|
| **Eph 1:4** | **Chosen to be** | **you will die** |
| **Heb 12:14** | **Without holiness** | **you will live** |
| **1 Pt 1:15-16** | **Be holy in all your conduct** | **no one will see the Lord** |
| **Rm 8:13** | **Live by the sinful nature** | **because God is holy** |
| **Rm 8:13** | **Live by the Spirit** | **holy and blameless** |

In *The Pursuit of Holiness*, Jerry Bridges writes, "Because we are not convinced of the deceitfulness of sin (Heb 3:13), we play with it, thinking we will thereby find satisfaction. And because we do not have a firm conviction that 'without holiness no one will see the Lord' (Heb 12:14), we do not seriously pursue holiness as a priority in our lives."

**Are you "convinced" regarding sin?**

**Are you "convicted" regarding holiness?**

**Is holiness a priority in your life?**

**Read Ephesians 5:3-4.**

**What are the six sins listed?**

______________________________________________

______________________________________________

**What reason does Paul give that saints should not participate in these sins?**

______________________________________________

The first two sins mentioned are sexual sins; then Paul mentions greed. The last three sins listed concern improper speech (obscenity, foolish talk, and vulgarity).

**Read 2 Corinthians 7:1.**

Pray, as Paul, to "walk in a manner worthy of the Lord, fully pleasing to Him, bearing fruit in every good work and increasing in the knowledge of God." (*Colossians 1:10, ESV*)

**What are we to do?**

______________________________________________

______________________________________________

**In what ways do you struggle with this?**

**What are some practical ways you can live that out in your life?**

When the Bible addresses sin and holiness, it uses strong language. It doesn't get much clearer than this: we are to bring "holiness to completion in the fear of God."

"Now you are light in the Lord. Walk as children of light" (Eph 5:8). We now walk away from the path of sin, in darkness, and walk the path of holiness, in His light. That is living by faith...this is walking prepared.

**Day 2**

# Walking the Path

Over lunch, my dear friend told me about her grand adventure touring Israel and Jordan. She traveled with her husband and a group led by Dr. Randall Price, an esteemed professor at Liberty University and previous Director of Excavations on the Qumran Plateau project. As I admired a particular photo in her prized album, she shared a fascinating story told by Mrs. Price.

In years past, their family had camped at the base of Tel Beth Shean. There were some ancient archeological discoveries in the vicinity at the time. Over the years, more and more of it has been unearthed; it has now become a major excavation site. Over the span of this project, archaeologists have uncovered the ancient ruins of Scytholopolis. As it turns out, the open field they used for a campsite was, in fact, over this ancient Roman city of the Decapolis. And the spot where they liked to pitch their tent (because it seemed the ground was more solid) was actually atop a 30' tall column!

In 749 A.D. an earthquake destroyed the city. Over time, the city was lost, as layer-upon-layer eventually buried it.

What was once prepared, then destroyed, was covered to look indistinguishable to what it once was. Beneath the layers lay ruins. But no one knew it. Only the new paths were known...*visible.*

To the naked eye we sometimes have no idea what ruins lie beneath the surface, once a new masterpiece is created in its place.

## The Path Paved with Compassion

As a prepared masterpiece, we are to walk a certain path...in a specific way.

Just as the yellow-brick road is paved with gold, the path of the Christian is paved with the gold of Christian virtues.

**Read from Ephesians 5:1-2 the way we are to walk.**

We are to walk in the way of love—as dearly loved children of the Most High God.

**Read Colossians 3:12-14.**

**What are we to wear?**

______________________________________________

______________________________________________

______________________________________________

We will spend the next few days of our journey unpacking this verse. We will discover how we are to walk this path of holiness—a path paved with the gold of love, compassion, humility, kindness, gentleness, patience and forgiveness. Today, let's look at compassion.

**Write Psalm 145:9.**

______________________________________________

______________________________________________

______________________________________________

"But you, Lord, are a compassionate and gracious God, slow to anger, abounding in love and faithfulness."
(*Psalm 86:15*)

**How is God referred to in 2 Corinthians 1:3?**

______________________________________________

**Who showed compassion in Mark 6:34?**

______________________________________________

**Read Nehemiah 9:17-28.**

**How many times is a form of compassion mentioned?**

____________________________________________

**What is the command of the Lord Almighty in Zechariah 7:9?**

____________________________________________

As we have already learned, God uses our experiences, circumstances, trials and suffering to prepare us—to teach faith lessons meant for us at that point in time. When we meet someone in a similar situation, that person doesn't need to hear about the lesson I learned. She merely needs to be met with compassion—with a loving touch. You may have learned firsthand that God turns suffering into blessing. That understanding is born from experience. From that experience, familiarity is born. And from that familiarity we are best able to recognize and relate to someone's pain so that we may administer compassion.

A compassionate touch stills the quaking within. It doesn't bring answers, solutions, victory, or even change. It often doesn't end the battle. It just helps the afflicted to feel that they are not fighting the battle alone. And in that, there is great comfort.

**Read Job 2:11-13.**

**How did they first respond, as recorded in these verses?**

____________________________________________

**How much talking was going on?** ____________________

Job's three friends are often criticized for the things they got wrong, but we should recognize those few things they did get right:

- They responded to a friend in need.
- They came to Job's side in his suffering.
- Their hearts were filled with genuine mourning and sorrow.

What lesson of application can we glean from these verses? These men best showed their compassion *prior to saying a word.*

**Do you struggle knowing what to say?**

______________________________________________

Compassion adds another set of footprints to the rocky path. It reassures the trepid navigator he doesn't travel that valley floor alone.

**Do you feel you have to fill the silence?**

______________________________________________

This is a valuable lesson for me, in realizing that there are occasions when it is best to remain silent. After all, who of us can truly understand suffering? It cannot be explained and, often, it is beyond our understanding. I certainly do not know the ways of God—none of us do!

Typically, I want to offer words of encouragement. But it is important for me to note that encouragement can be silent. Comfort is given in our presence...our prayers...our compassion.

We can extend compassion, no matter what lies in our past. Regardless of the layers of ruins God may have used to prepare us, He can create a beautiful path for us to walk compassionately.

Day 3

# A Path Paved With Virtue

"A wise woman who was traveling in the mountains found a precious stone in a stream.

"The next day she met another traveler who was hungry, so she opened her bag to share her food. The hungry traveler saw the precious stone and asked the woman for it. She didn't hesitate in giving it to him.

"The traveler left, rejoicing in his good fortune. He knew the stone was worth enough for a lifetime of security. But after a few days, he came back and returned the stone to the woman.

"'I've been thinking,' he said. 'I know how valuable this stone is, but I am giving it back, hoping you will give me something even more precious.' 'What is that?' replied the woman. 'Give me what you have within you that enabled you to give it away.'

"It's not worldly wealth you possess, but the treasure inside that others need most."

"Kindness that is aware of itself has lost much of its charm."

*~J. R. Miller*

I came across this parable many years ago. The date and author may be unknown to me, but the lesson makes a lasting impression—because it's so true!

The lovingkindness we express to others is of greater value than anything else we can give away.

**Look at Colossians 3:12 below and circle those things we are to wear as we walk this path of Christ discipleship.**

**"Therefore, as God's chosen people, holy and dearly loved, clothe yourselves with compassion, kindness, humility, gentleness and patience."**

We only have time to touch briefly on three today. We'll examine humility tomorrow.

## The Path of Kindness, Gentleness and Patience

All of these attributes are unique yet interdependent. It's hard to be kind without a gentle heart. And it's difficult to be gentle without humility. But it's impossible for any without love.

Because they often appear so similar, sometimes it's hard to tell them apart. Maybe an exercise in contrasts will help.

**Match the opposites:**

| | |
|---|---|
| **Kindness** | **Harshness** |
| **Gentleness** | **Short-tempered** |
| **Patience** | **Meanness** |

"Patience implies suffering, enduring or waiting, as a determination of the will and not simply under necessity."

~*W. L. Walker* (*Standard Bible Encyclopedia*)

**From the selected readings below determine whether it is an example of gentleness, patience or kindness:**

**2 Samuel 9:1-13**

**David showed** ________________

**John 8:1-11**

**Jesus showed** ________________

**Judges 2:16-19**

**God showed** ________________

God has exhibited such kindness, gentleness, and patience toward us. And He continues to do so. It's this of His heart He intends to be visible in the masterpiece He is creating in us.

**Read Luke 6:35-36.**

**Which attributes of kindness, gentleness and patience are necessary in these actions given by Jesus to love our enemies?**

"Gentleness includes true humility that does not consider itself too good or too exalted for humble tasks."
*~Stanley M. Horton*

______________________________

______________________________

**What other virtue does He mention?**

______________________________

I read in the *Evangelical Dictionary of Biblical Theology* on kindness: "An attribute of God and quality desirable but not consistently found in humans." Ouch! Truth stabs, doesn't it? It just goes to show that since we struggle in exhibiting these qualities, we should then be patient and forgiving when others struggle in the same areas we do.

**Which do you struggle with most?**

______________________________

______________________________

**But what do you have that makes it possible?**

______________________________

Day 4

## A Lowliness of Mind

Our final stop as we learn to walk the Colossians 3:12 path is humility. But, really, it all **starts** with humility. For it is in this posture that we come into the presence of the holy, omnipotent majesty of Jehovah-God. We have a healthy opinion of ourselves when we acknowledge our state, station and utterly dependent position before Him. Only when we bow to the preeminent authority of Jesus as Master and Lord (see Eph. 1:21 and Heb. 2:8) is our attitude properly tuned.

"Humility is indeed a virtue.... It is the spontaneous recognition of the creature's absolute dependence on his Creator.

"It is the attitude which results from a fearlessly honest self-appraisal, a self-appraisal which neither minimizes one's achievements nor exaggerates one's failures."

(*Bible Gateway Study Tools, Encyclopedia of the Bible*)

**One sure reason to be humble is found in 1 John 1:8-10; which is:**

________________________________________

**What reasons do you find for humility in these two passages in Isaiah?**

**Isaiah 57:15** ______________________________

________________________________________

**Isaiah 66:1-2** ______________________________

________________________________________

In humility, we acknowledge that all that we are, all that we do, all that we have is from God Almighty. In that humble state we then come to fully realize that salvation is purely of God's grace, not our works.

Nonetheless, there is something we *are* to do...

**What similar instruction do you find in 1 Peter 3:8 and 1 Peter 5:5?**

________________________________________

## More on Becoming Less

The Greek word for humility (*tapeinótita*) is a combination of two words that can literally be translated as a "lowliness of mind."

So just how are we to have such a lowliness of mind?

**Circle the admonition found in:**

**Romans 12:3:**

**Think highly of yourself**

**Think of yourself with sober judgment**

**Degrade yourself**

**Philippians 2:3:**

**Value others above yourself**

**Value yourself above others**

**Value others opinion of you**

**Matthew 20:25-28**

**Exercise your authority over others**

**Strive to be first**

**Have the mindset of a servant**

The golden key buried in those verses is to make more of others…to make others more—more of them and less of me.

**From Matthew 20:25-28, what does Jesus tell us about how to be humble?**

________________________________________

It's all well and good to read about humility, but if you're anything like me, it helps to see it in action. The Bible offers several examples.

**Match the humble one with the passage:**

| | |
|---|---|
| **Jesus** | **Mk 1:7** |
| **John, the Baptist** | **Rev 1:17** |
| **John, the Apostle** | **Lk 17:7-10** |
| **Servants** | **Mt 11:29-30** |

The ministries of John, the Baptist and Jesus overlapped. While John only wanted to lead people to Jesus (see Jn 1:6-8, 23; Jn 3:30), his followers had two attitudes that make humility near impossible: comparison and competition. Other killers to humility? Envy and jealousy.

"Humility opens the way to all other godly character traits. It is the soil in which the other traits of the fruit of the Spirit grow."

*~Jerry Bridges (The Practice of Godliness)*

**When the competition arose, see how John handled it from John 3:27.**

**How have you seen either of these hinder your ability to remain humble?**

______________________________________________

To be humble is to have the opposite attitude of the Pharisee depicted in Luke 18:9. May I just confess right here that I have known a similar pride!

Humility is not a Fruit of the Spirit (as are others we've mentioned this week). We must first cooperate with the Holy Spirit in humility. When we bow in submission and surrender, He provides the other fruit and is able to work in and through us.

I love the advice of Kenneth Kirk: "Worship alone can make us humble." That is where He really prepares us most—in humble worship.

As we walk this path of good works God has prepared in advance for us to do, let it be a path paved with humility, patience, gentleness, and compassion.

Day 5

# Bringing God Praise

The petal does it for the flower;
The feather to the bird;
The garden for the farmer;
The children to the parents.

Do we?

As God's creatures, do we bring praise to God, our Father?

Oh, there's the fruit of our lips that gives God praise. But do our actions—our lives—bring God praise?

They should.

Bringing God praise is how we should walk and work, as His prepared.

## Praise for the Altogether Praiseworthy

Let's see what we can see today, friends.

**Read Galatians 1:22-24.**

**What was the response after Paul reported the work God had done in him?**

______________________________________________

**Read Acts 21:17-20.**

**What was the response after Paul reported what God had been doing through Paul's work?**

______________________________________________

"Nothing I can do, Nothing I bring, is worthy of Your love to me. This life I have to live is all I have to give. So Lord, do what you want to do with me. Just let my life bring praise to You; let my life bring You praise." Let My Life Bring You Praise

*~Gary Mott*

**Read Ephesians 1:11-14.**

**What is God's will for the first to hope in Christ**

**(vs 12)?**____________________________________

**Write out our purpose, as stated in Isaiah 43:21.**

________________________________________________

________________________________________________

________________________________________________

**What are your findings in 1 Peter 2:9?**

________________________________________________

**Fill in the blanks from the word bank from 1 Peter 4:11.**

**WORD BANK**

| | |
|---|---|
| **ALL** | **GOD** |
| **PRAISED** | **SERVES** |
| **STRENGTH** | |

**If anyone** ____________________**, he should do it with the**

________________________ __________________________

**provides, so that in** _________________**things God may be**

______________________**through Jesus Christ.**

When we serve with the strength God provides, He is seen and therefore the One to be praised. And Paul's life exemplified this principle.

**How is this put into practice?**

______________________________________________

______________________________________________

**Read 2 Corinthians 9:13 from the sidebar.**

**What would cause others to praise God?**

______________________________________________

"Because of the service by which you have proved yourselves, others will praise God for the obedience that accompanies your confession of the gospel of Christ, and for your generosity in sharing with them and with everyone else."

(*2 Corinthians 9:13*)

Because of Paul's obedience, his life brought God praise. And because He believed the invisible God to be all he praised Him for, his life couldn't help but reflect God and bring Him into view.

Living to bring praise to an altogether praiseworthy God gives rich meaning, purpose, and satisfaction to this one, precious life.

And when we walk the path God has prepared for us in the manner we've studied this week, our lives will bring Him praise—and we will be able to say with Paul...

**Prepared to Say**

"I can do all things through Him Who gives me strength" (Php 4:13).

*WEEK TEN*

# Prepared to Finish

**DAY 1**

## Shipwrecked

You're here: Week 10! I commend you for your stick-to-itiveness. I prayed for you at the beginning, and I'm praying even harder now that we're heading down the home stretch. Our days to study together may be numbered and dwindling, but they are packed with major topics before we close out our time together.

As we have seen, God prepares us. He never abandons us and He never stops preparing us. He prepares us for works...and He prepares us to finish.

Just look at Paul...

Perseverance is "maintaining Christian faith through the trying times of life.

"The background setting for the idea of perseverance blossomed out of the context of persecution and temptation."

The New Testament writers "believed Christians would finish the race because Christians would focus their attention on Jesus, the lead runner and model finisher of their faith.

"Perseverance is thus a call to faithfulness."

*~Gerald L. Borchert*
*Holman Illustrated Bible Dictionary*

**What is Paul's instruction in 2 Corinthians 8:11?**

______________________________________________

**What is the encouragement for us found in Hebrews 10:36?**

______________________________________________

**Write Romans 12:11.**

______________________________________________

______________________________________________

**Name a time when it was hard for you to "keep your spiritual fervor."**

______________________________________________

# Paul's Enduring Faith

Paul endured more than any one man I know: hungry and homeless, persecuted and stoned, chained and imprisoned, and nearly drowned. No matter how many times Paul was shipwrecked, his trials never shipwrecked his faith. And no matter how many times he found himself in chains, he never lost his freedom in Christ. He may have been imprisoned, but the Spirit swelled and soared within him.

**Read Acts 20:17-24.**

**Check Paul's work among the Ephesians.**
(Place a check mark next to the statement that applies, as found in verses 18-21.)

| | |
|---|---|
| | **Served the Lord with humility** |
| | **Tested by plotting Jews** |
| | **Preached what was helpful** |
| | **Taught from house to house** |
| | **Declared repentance and faith in Jesus** |

**From verse 23, how was Paul prepared for what he faced?**

___________________________________________

**What were his two ambitions (stated in verse 24)?**

- __________**the race**
- __________**to the gospel of God's grace**

In the face of great peril Paul did not fear, but was determined to complete the task to which he was called. On more than one occasion he received a timely word of encouragement from the Lord that helped him to press on (Acts 18:9; 27:24). He encouraged the other passengers aboard a sinking ship with these words: "Take heart."

"I have told you these things, so that in Me you may have peace. In this world you will have trouble. But take heart! I have overcome the world."
(*John 16:33*)

**John 16:33 records these same words of encouragement from Whom?**

________________________________________________

**Where is peace found?**

________________________________________________

**What does the world offer?**

________________________________________________

**But Jesus** ________________________________________

**the** ____________________.

(Fill in the blanks above from John 16:33b in the sidebar.)

We can get tossed around from the rough storms of this life—shipwrecked, even. But be confident in this: God has prepared us to finish. So "take heart," dear saint. Endure to the end—anchored to hope—and you will receive God's promised reward.

## Day 2
# Unfinished

The Bible is filled with heart-rending stories that ended sadly of people who had such promise and potential. People who started strong, only to come to a tragic end. By studying the choices that led to their downfall, we can hopefully learn what to avoid so that we may finish well. That's where we'll tread the rest of the week.

First up: Gideon, a warrior gone wrong.

## Gideon's Less Than Valiant Finish

**Read the backdrop from Judges 6:1-6.**

**Below, underline what Gideon was doing.**

**Circle what the angel called him.**

"The angel of the LORD came and sat down under the oak in Ophrah that belonged to Joash the Abiezrite, where his son Gideon was threshing wheat in a winepress to keep it from the Midianites. When the angel of the LORD appeared to Gideon, he said, 'The LORD is with you, mighty warrior.'" (Jgs 6:11-12)

A mighty warrior hiding in a winepress? That doesn't quite fit, now does it?

**Describe a time when your behavior didn't align with how God sees you.**

______________________________________________

______________________________________________

______________________________________________

Gideon had many questions for God. But in patiently answering them, God prepared Gideon to obey God's call.

**Read Judges 6:13-16.**

**What was Gideon told he would do (vs 14)?**

______________________________________________

**What was his assurance (vs 16)?**

______________________________________________

**Judges 6:25-26 assigns his first order of business, which**

**is:** ____________________________________________

______________________________________________

His first act of deliverance from idol worship earned Gideon a new name: Baal Fighter.

**We learn in Judges 6:34 that Gideon's battle armor is:**
**A B C D**

**A) Gilded helmet and sword**

**B) Ornamented breastplate**

**C) The Spirit**

**D) Newly shod boots**

**Before they headed into battle, God pruned the Israelite army to a ratio of 450:1; for what obvious reason (see Jgs 7:2)?**

______________________________________________

**According to Judges 7:16, what three weapons did they have?**

**1)** ________________________________________

**2)** ________________________________________

**3)** ________________________________________

**What weapons do we have in "battle"?**

______________________________________________

**Jump ahead now to Judges 7:22. Who deserved credit for the victory?**

__________________________________________________

**But, from Judges 8:22, who got it?**

__________________________________________________

**Look to Deuteronomy 8:14 to see what God has warned of prideful forgetfulness.**

"Whenever we take what God has done and put it in the place of Himself, we become idolaters."

~ *Oswald Chambers* (*The Westminster Collection of Christian Quotes*)

Gideon was armored by the Holy Spirit. And to prove beyonda-shadow of every doubt that the victory was His, God increased the army ratio in favor of the enemy by a ridiculously disproportionate amount. The only hope for the Israelites' victory was their complete obedience and reliance upon God.

God was the clear Victor that day, however Gideon got the credit. Pride is, indeed, a most destructive force that inevitably leads to our downfall. And we will see how it kept Gideon from a valiant finish.

In reading the rest of Gideon's story through Judges 8, a departure from God's leading seems apparent. Where the "Spirit of the Lord" came upon Gideon to gather the troops (Jgs 6:34-35), Gideon seems to summon them himself (Jgs 7:23-24). These are likely the same men God dismissed in the pruning process conducted earlier. Gideon went beyond the bounds assigned to him by God prior to the Midianite battle by reassembling more troops for the chase.

The troops pressed on—weary, hungry, and exhausted—another 25 miles to Karkor (Jgs 8:4).

**Recall a time you were spent but pushed on...pursuing. What helped you finish?**

__________________________________________________

__________________________________________________

**What do you make of Gideon's remark in Judges 8:7?**

________________________________________

**What of his threat in Judges 8:8-9?**

________________________________________

**Read Judges 8:10-17.**

Gideon not only tears down the Peniel tower (8:9), he massacres the leaders (8:17). Does Gideon still seem "on track" in doing the will of God?

**Read Judges 8:18-21.**

**What is his driving motivation in the execution of Zebah and Zalmunna (vs 19)?**

________________________________________

Gideon doesn't appear to be seeking direction from God, as he once did.

When he returns from battle, the Israelites are determined to now worship him as their ruler. Gideon does make the comment that God is the true Ruler of the people (Jgs 8:23), but he doesn't set the record straight about Who their real Deliverer is. They gave Gideon glory that belonged to God...and Gideon did not correct them.

**Read Judges 8:24-27.**

**What actions are recorded in verse 27?**

________________________________________

We don't know Gideon's intentions for the ephod, but we don't hear it as commanded by God. And, more importantly, it clearly became a snare for the people (likely Gideon included).

Gideon may have verbally rejected their offer to be their ruler, but his actions prove otherwise (vs 24-31). He was ornamented as a king, wore purple garments, lived as a king, collected a king's offerings, and assembled a harem. But far worse than any of that, he led the nation back to the idolatry he was first told to abolish by *becoming the idol*.

Gideon was the warrior of valor in the battle against the Midianites, but the victory of war was spoiled when he stopped following God. Pride and plunder further tainted his finish as the idol he created stole the hearts of the people and turned them away from their Deliverer yet again.

We learn several things from Gideon. We learn that when God has secured the victory and we step from the battlefield we have to keep looking to God and keep pointing others to Him. When we stop looking to God we fail to finish.

So, to finish, then, is to remain: remain humble, remain free from idolatry, and remain obedient.

"You shall have no other gods before Me. You shall not make for yourself a carved image, or any likeness of anything that is in heaven above, or that is in the earth beneath, or that is in the water under the earth. You shall not bow down to them or worship them, for I the LORD your God am a jealous God, visiting the iniquity of the fathers on the children to the third and the fourth generation of those who hate Me."

(*Exodus 20:3-5, ESV*)

Day 3

## A Lesson from King Saul

There are those who have a strong start…only to have a failed finish. Sad…but true. It can be quite helpful sometimes to learn not only what to do, by looking at what works in the lives of others, but also to look at what not to do.

Today, we look at the "what-not-tos" in finishing well from the account of Saul, Israel's first king.

"Saul was thirty years old when he became king, and he reigned over Israel forty-two years."
(*1 Samuel 13:1*)

**Read 1 Samuel 9:15-17.**

**What is God's stated purpose for choosing Saul (vs 16)?**

______________________________________________

**From 1 Samuel 9:21, what similarities do you see in Saul's response compared with where the angel found Gideon?**

______________________________________________

Gideon was hiding in a winepress. Saul was hiding amid the baggage (1 Sm 9: 21-22). Adam and Eve hid in the brush. Jonah hid on a ship. Peter hid outside the city gate.

**Have you ever tried to "hide" from God? Explain:**

______________________________________________

**Read 1 Samuel 10:24.**

**What kind of start does King Saul have?**

______________________________________________

**Read 1 Samuel 11:11.**

**How did his army fare under his command in his first battle against the Ammonites?**

______________________________

Saul and his wife Ahinoam had five sons and two daughters. His oldest son Jonathan was David's friend. Saul's daughter, Michal was David's wife—making Saul David's father-in-law.

**From 1 Samuel 11:13, to Whom did he give credit?**

______________________________

**What is read favorably of him in 1 Samuel 14:28?**

______________________________

Now we'll fast-forward to his battle against the Amalekites. Samuel delivered God's command for Saul to attack and completely destroy all that belonged to the Amalekites (1 Sm 15:1-3). However, Saul spared King Agag and took the best of the cattle and possessions as plunder (1 Sm 15:9). In Samuel's confrontation with him, he compounds his disobedience with a lie.

**Pick up in their conversation by reading from 1 Samuel 15:17-19.**

**What attitude does "small in your own eyes" indicate?**

______________________________

**What reason does Samuel give for Saul being rejected by God (vs 19)?**

______________________________

**Saul stated in verse 21 that he took the plunder in order to sacrifice them to...**

- ☐ **The Lord my God**
- ☐ **The Lord your God**

**Read 1 Samuel 15:22-23.**

**What is the equivalence to arrogance noted in verse 23?**

______________________________________________

**Read Matthew 10:32-33. Note any similarities you see with 1 Samuel 15:23b:**

______________________________________________

Although Saul was once humble, he grew arrogant...to such a degree that he wouldn't even acknowledge God to be *his* Lord. God was terribly grieved by Saul's actions and rejected him as king.

Skip ahead to the battle against the Philistines, those from whom he was chosen to deliver God's people. At this point Samuel is gone and Saul is full of fear, so he consults a medium.

One of the most troubling verses in all of Scripture is 1 Samuel 16:14:

"Now the Spirit of the LORD had departed from Saul, and an evil spirit from the LORD tormented him."

**What does Samuel's spirit tell him has happened in 1 Samuel 28:16?**

______________________________________________

**What reason does he give in verse 18?**

______________________________________________

**Read of Saul's end from 1 Samuel 31:1-6.**

Disobedience was King Saul's downfall. His heart never belonged to God. It would seem that many of the decisions he made in leading God's people stemmed either from fear or arrogance. Then, once rejected by God, he lived a deeply troubled life.

Our disobedience does not have to end in our demise—not if we humble ourselves and return to the Lord.

**Write the good news of the restoration we have in Jesus from Romans 5:19:**

______________________________________________

______________________________________________

**Day 4**

## A Riches-to-Rags Tale

Who doesn't like a good story? You know the ones: tales with happy endings, stories in which the underdog wins or justice prevails. Everyone loves a good rags-to-riches story.

When we hear of someone who has ridden on the wings of success only to crash in a heap, we are left puzzled and perplexed. It's the riches-to-rags tales that cause our stomachs to turn and our heads to shake.

## A Royal Mess

When royalty fall from their thrones, it's a hard landing…smack dab in the middle of a royal mess. Meet our royal subject of the day: King Uzziah. Turn with me to his story in 2 Chronicles 26.

**Read 2 Chronicles 26:1-5.**

**Fill in the blank from verse 4:**

**He did** ______________________________

**in the eyes of the Lord.**

**According to verse 5, how did Zechariah instruct him?**

_________________________________________________________

**Read verses 6-8 and note what he became:**

____________________________________ **(vs 8)**

**Make a list of accomplishments noted in verses 9-15:**

_________________________________________________________

_________________________________________________________

_________________________________________________________

King Uzziah was the tenth king of Judah. "Uzziah" was his throne name. He is called by his personal name in 1 Kings 15 as "Azariah."

"Uzziah was sixteen years old when he became king, and he reigned in Jerusalem fifty-two years. His mother's name was Jekoliah; she was from Jerusalem."

(*2 Chron 26:3*)

"Success is not final,
failure is not fatal:
It is the courage to
continue that counts."

*~Winston Churchill*

**Would you consider him successful?**

______________________________________________

**How do you define success?**

______________________________________________

______________________________________________

**Is any success pulling you away from God?**

______________________________________________

**What's the three-letter warning word that opens verse 16?** ________ ________ ________

**Write out verse 16.**

______________________________________________

______________________________________________

**How can success become a snare?**

______________________________________________

**Read verse 17-23.**

**What was wrong with what he did (vs 18)?**

______________________________________________

**How did he react (vs 19)?** ______________________

**What was the outcome?** ______________________________

**How did he get it (vs 20)?** ___________________________

God blessed King Uzziah to ride the heights of success "until he became strong"—until he pridefully began to trust in self over God. Success became his downfall because it became **his** success.

The day Uzziah overstepped his authority was the day God could no longer leave him undisciplined. He acted as if he were above the law by usurping the priestly duties of burning the incense. This was an act God could not ignore. Struck with leprosy, he had to relinquish his royal duties to his son, Jotham. He was also banned from the temple and forced to live separate from others the rest of his days.

After his death he was not remembered for his earlier fame and accomplishments. Rather, he was known as leprous.

**How do you want to be remembered?**

_____________________________________________________

_____________________________________________________

"Pride leads to every other vice; it is the complete anti-God state of mind."

~ *C. S. Lewis*

Just because Uzziah was king, and just because he had a string of accomplishments, they did not make him immune from consequences of pride. His success came from the only King that deserves to be exalted and enthroned on high. His failure to acknowledge that kept him from finishing well.

Part of our finishing is to remain humble. One sure way to help us do so is to pray daily for humility. We can start today by praying Proverbs 30:9:

**Write out your own prayer by personalizing Proverbs 30:9:**

_____________________________________________________

_____________________________________________________

_____________________________________________________

Day 5

# From Whence Comes a King's Help

Not only did King Asa have double "As" in his name, he had two "As" on his performance review for doing both "good and right."

## Looking for Help in All the Wrong Places

Much of King Asa's reign enjoyed peace. Let's see why.

"Large numbers had come over to [Asa] from Israel when they saw that the LORD his God was with him. They assembled at Jerusalem in the third month of the fifteenth year of Asa's reign. At that time they sacrificed to the LORD seven hundred head of cattle and seven thousand sheep and goats from the plunder they had brought back. They entered into a covenant to seek the LORD, the God of their ancestors, with all their heart and soul. All Judah rejoiced about the oath because they had sworn it wholeheartedly. They sought God eagerly, and He was found by them. So the LORD gave them rest on every side."

*(2 Chron 15:9b-12, 15)*

**Read 2 Chronicles 14:2.**

**Check the correct ending to this sentence:**

**Asa did good and right**

- ☐ **in his own eyes**
- ☐ **in the eyes of the people**
- ☐ **in the eyes of the Lord**

It is further stated in 1 Kings 15 that his heart was fully committed to the Lord (1 Kg 15:14b).

**Second Chronicles 14:3-5 lists some of the things he did that earned the description of "good and right." What are they?**

________________________________________

________________________________________

**What are some other successes mentioned in verses 6-8?**

________________________________________

________________________________________

**What did the Lord grant them, according to verses 6 and 7?** ______________________

**Read 2 Chronicles 14:9-12.**

**Upon whom did they call for victory?**

______________________

Did you know that Asa is in the lineage of Jesus and that Jehoshaphat is his son?

Check it out in Matthew 1:7.

**Write out his prayer from verse 11.**

______________________

______________________

______________________

**Is that a passage worthy of memorizing so that you may use it in your own prayers?**

______________________

**Who struck down the Cushites?** ______________________

**What is God's warning in 2 Chronicles 15:2?**

______________________

God blessed Judah under the obedient leadership of King Asa with ten years of prosperity and peace. When the Cushites marched out against Judah, they called upon the Lord and He crushed their enemy. Filled with the Spirit, the prophet Azariah met the king with a promising word from the Lord. King Asa and the people responded with a great revival and wholeheartedly renewed their covenant with God. They then enjoyed another 20 years of peace.

**What else did King Asa do, according to 2 Chronicles 15:18?**

______________________

**Read 2 Chronicles 16:1-3.**

**Where did he seek help when King Baasha of Israel invaded?**

____________________________________________

**What did Asa give to the King of Aram (vs 2)?**

____________________________________________

King Asa sought God for victory against the Cushites (2 Chron 14:11) but sought out Ben-Hadad for help against Israel. The gold and silver he first gave to God, he then took back to give to another. And he traded his covenant with God for a treaty with man. The trust and allegiance he once held for God he reassigned to man.

The reason we can conclude that King Asa did not finish well is because of the explanation given through Hanani, the prophet.

**Read 2 Chronicles 16:7-8.**

**What was the pivotal turning point for King Asa, as stated by Hanani?**

____________________________________________

**According to verse 9, did God want to bless Asa?**

____________________________________________

**(Look to 1 Kg 15:14 if you need help in answering this question.)**

**What is the condition?** __________________________

**What is Asa's response given in verse 10?**

____________________________________________

Asa becomes enraged with Hanani, the servant of God. He unjustly imprisons him for speaking God's truth. When confronted, he refused correction and compounded the wrong by brutally oppressing the people. What would have happened had he admitted to God he was wrong?

Sometimes God sends someone into our lives to correct us with a truthful word of instruction to bring us back to Him.

**We have a choice in the way we can respond.**
**Which one is best?**

**Rebel**

**Reject**

**Resent**

**Rage**

**Repent**

**Rationalize**

"It is better to trust in the LORD than to put confidence in man." (*Psalm 118:8 NKJV*)

**Read 2 Chronicles 16:12-13.**

**Complete verse 12:**

**Though his disease was severe, even in his**

**illness he** ______________________________

**but only** ______________________________**.**

Where King Asa once sought help from God and trusted Him, at some point he began to trust man. There are times when we get help from our fellow man, as in getting medical attention when we become ill, but we must always seek God and trust in Him.

As long as Asa was obedient to God, he had peace with God. It was when he did not heed Azariah's warning (2 Chronicles 15:2), that he forfeited an honorable finish.

Learning from the "what-not-tos" this week was just as helpful as studying what *to do* in finishing our walk as the prepared of God. We saw where Gideon stopped following God and led the people back into idolatry. We learned that Saul's downfall came from his disobedience. The success of Uzziah made him self-reliant. And King Asa relinquished his trust in God for trust in man. But they all had one thing in common: pride—the downfall of us all.

Remaining humble helps us to finish...and finish well. By holding tightly to the unshakeable conviction of the trustworthiness of God and the gospel of Christ, we become prepared to say.

**Prepared to Say**

"I know Whom I have believed, and am convinced that He is able to guard what I have entrusted to Him until that day" (2 Tm 1:12b).

*WEEK ELEVEN*

# Finishing Strong

**DAY 1**

## Bewares and Snares

Here's an encouraging word for you, sister: Our Creator God is recreating a new you—a masterpiece. Not a masterpiece to set on a pedestal. No! Much more noble than that. He wants you to work, prepared. He wants you to walk, prepared. And He doesn't prepare works in advance for you merely to *cruise* along (or worse, stall out!). He doesn't want you to *just* finish—*coasting* across the finish line. No! Rather, He wants you to finish well...to *finish **strong***.

**What does it mean to you to finish strong?**

________________________________________

________________________________________

**Complete Hebrews 3:14:**

**We know we share in Christ if we hold our original conviction**

________________________________________

________________________________________

"Living well matters. Ending well matters even more."
*~Liz Curtis-Higgs*

## Admonishments

We learn both by instruction and example (even bad example, as we discovered last week). The New Testament is full of "bewares" and "snares"—warnings and admonishments that help us avoid the dangers that threaten to rob us of a strong finish.

**According to Acts 20:23, what was the Source of Paul's warnings?**

________________________________________

"He will also keep you firm to the end, so that you will be blameless on the day of our Lord Jesus Christ."

(*1 Corinthians 1:8*)

**Of what snares does the Spirit make us aware in 1 Timothy 4:1-2?**

______________________________________________

______________________________________________

**Paul states the reason he wrote the letter to the Corinthians. It can be found in 1 Corinthians 4:14:**

______________________________________________

**What is the warning in Hebrews 2:1?**

______________________________________________

**What follows the "so that"?**

______________________________________________

Paul wrote his letter to the Corinthians as a means to warn them. Even David has told us that heeding the warnings found in God's decrees has great reward (Ps 19:11). These have been written so that we do not drift from our faith.

**Read 1 Timothyw 6:17-19.**

**What two dangers are noted in verse 17?**

**1)** ______________________________________

**2)** ______________________________________

**What can we do to counter these dangers?**

______________________________________________

______________________________________________

**Complete the conclusion of verse 19:**

**Take hold of life that is** ___________________________

Paul teaches us that pride, wealth, liars, and false teachings are huge snares to avoid. He wrote of other snares to beware to the Galatians.

**Read Galatians 3:1-3.**

**What is a caution given in verse 3?**

______________________________________________

We started our walk with the Spirit, and we must finish our earthly walk in the Spirit, not turning away to rely upon our flesh.

**Complete the urgings found in 1 Thessalonians 5:14:**

**W** ______________________________

**E** ______________________________

**H** ______________________________

**B** ______________________________

**Remember, what you read on the other side of a "so that" speaks to purpose. So then, according to Colossians 1:28, what is the purpose of admonishment?**

______________________________________________

If we are to finish this walk of faith strong, we must allow the Spirit to continue to do the work of maturing us in Christ. Growing on to maturity often includes some necessary and beneficial admonishments along the way. As Paul told the Thessalonians, those in the Lord admonish because they care (1 Thes 5:12); which should be our only motive behind it, as well.

Although forewarned, we are not always forearmed. We may be aware of certain, harmful snares and still find ourselves entangled in the consequences of willful sin. Though warnings abound, we sometimes have to learn the hard way—from firsthand experience...of the wrong kind. Thankfully, God has provided a remedy.

**Write 1 John 1:9.**

______________________________________________

______________________________________________

The grace God extended to us for the forgiveness of our sins at the first is the same grace He continues to extend to us throughout. He has also graciously given us His Word to keep us strong, to keep us close, and to keep truth before us. Abiding in the Word will enable us to remain aware and alert in the presence of danger—because "in these last days, many will fall away." But warnings and admonishments will keep us on track... to the finish.

*Noutheteite* is the Greek word translated as "admonish." It is a present, imperative, active verb which means: "appeal to the mind; counsel; warn; exhort."

*Strong's Concordance* provides that it is "to reprove gently, not chastise."

*HELP Word Studies* states it is "reasoning with someone by warning" and "urging them to choose God's best."

## How To Finish

The faith-life of the Christian is forward moving. It is meant to be ever advancing toward a goal.

**Place the correct verbs in the blanks from the statement Paul made in Philippians 3:13:**

**______________what is behind and**

**______________toward what is ahead.**

There should be no looking back for the Christian. (You can't advance if you're chained to the past.) We are to be ever pressing onward.

**Write out Philippians 3:12:**

____________________________________________

____________________________________________

____________________________________________

Paul never felt he had "arrived." And neither should we. He desperately wanted what Jesus wanted for him. He wanted to possess that for which Jesus seized hold of him.

Let's look at some other powerful verbs from the pen of Paul.

**Read 1 Timothy 6:11-16.**

**What are two words of action used in verse 11?**

**1)** ______________________________________

**2)** ______________________________________

**What implored actions are in verse 12?**

1) ______________________________

2) ______________________________

Advancing toward our goal is to take hold of eternal life, to flee from ungodliness and pursue righteousness.

**What else are we to pursue (vs 11)?**

______________________________

______________________________

There are indeed those things we are to do as we are walking, working, and growing. But we must always remember Who keeps us moving.

## Whose Strength Is It Anyway?

The hail storm mercilessly beat down my newly planted Rose of Sharon. It looked pitiful—the sagging sapling all bowed low in surrender. The one next to it seemed quite sufficient, a dependable source of strength. So I tied it to the stronger one for support. It seemed a parable of sorts: that I should bind myself to the All-Sufficient God instead of striving to rely on my own frailties—especially when feeling beaten down by the troubles of this world. Augustine of Hippo wrote, "When God is our strength, it is strength indeed; when our strength is our own, it is only weakness."

**Are you allowing God to make you stronger? Do you rely on His strength or try to muster up your own when you feel weak?**

______________________________

______________________________

"The greatness of a man's power is the measure of his surrender."
*~William Booth*

**What is it that makes you feel weak?**

______________________________

**Where do you need His strength today?**

__________________________________________

My little sapling didn't have the strength to stand on its own. It was reliant upon another for strength and stability. It took time and care to eventually thrive. But until it grew and became stronger, it needed to be yoked to one more sufficient.

**Read 1 Peter 1:3-5.**

**Circle below what it is that keeps you until the "last time" (from verse 5 of the NKJV):**

**"who are kept by the power of God through faith for salvation ready to be revealed in the last time."**

The Old Testament records several examples of what mortal man could do when the power of the Holy Spirit came upon them. Samson (Jgs 14:6), David (1 Sm 16:13), even Saul (1 Sm 11:6ff) were only able to accomplish by the strength provided by the Holy Spirit. And let's not overlook the disciples at Pentecost and the vibrant growth of the church under the divine power of the Holy Spirit recorded in the Book of Acts.

"Sing about a fruitful vineyard: I, the LORD, watch over it; I water it continually. I guard it day and night so that no one may harm it."

(*Isaiah 27:2-3*)

**What actions of God follows the "I" in Isaiah 27:2-3 in the sidebar?"**

**I** ____________________________________

**I** ____________________________________

**I** ____________________________________

We finish strong when we finish out our faith-life in a God-pleasing way—ever advancing toward God's goal, fulfilling God's purpose, under God's direction, by the power of God.

This year in our Ladies' Class, we will be covering the workbook Prepared, by Debbra Stephens. The lessons are broken up a little different than what we are used to, so I wanted to give everyone a little more information.

The book is divided into "weeks" (lessons). Each week is divided into 5 days. It breaks the lesson up so you are able to study a little bit each day of the week, instead of covering everything all at once. That gives you an opportunity to focus and study each topic a little more deeply. I know that sounds a little intimidating, but don't worry! The days are short and filled with questions to answer and thoughts to reflect on. We will be going over one week (lesson) a month.

There will be no assigned teacher for each lesson like we have done in the past. We will all just come together and discuss what we have studied over the course of the last month. If time permits, we may read through the lesson together also. So don't be hindered from coming if you haven't done the lesson or if you don't have your book! We will be meeting each second Tuesday of the month at Panera Bread on Vann Drive at 6:30 pm.

I am looking forward to this year trying something new with all you ladies while we study God's word and learn that God prepares us for what He has prepared for us!

Please see Katie Angel if you have any questions.

## Day 3
# An Enduring Finish

There is a story of a runner who started a race with high hopes of winning. He started in the lead, only to stumble and fall a few yards out of the blocks. The crowd laughed and jeered but hope got him up and running again. It was much too early in the race to be defeated, he thought.

Distracted, he slipped and fell again. Scoffers jeered, and others tried to make him believe it was a lost cause. The louder voice in the crowd came from his father, urging him not to quit.

Discouraged, he rose again and tried to find his stride. He tried too hard and ran too fast, going down yet again.

Committed not to disappoint his father, he got up and carried on, realizing that not winning was not the same as failing. Time and again he got up and carried on. And then he heard a small voice cheer: "Winning is to rise every time you fall."

Three times he fell...three times he rose. He ran to the end, and he finished the race. Meeting up with his father on the other side of the finish line, he sadly admitted loss. "To me you won," his father replied, "all you have to do to win is rise one more time than you fall, until the race is done."

The Bible uses race metaphors often when referring to the endurance of our faith. The *New International Encyclopedia of Bible Words* has this to say on endurance: "The New Testament terms especially suggest patient waiting, but they do not imply passivity. [Endurance] is inspired by hope. Although it is God who gives endurance, patient endurance remains one of the virtues by which Christian character can be measured."

## It's a Matter of Keeping

Let's look to the admonition of the writer of the Book of Hebrews for a better understanding of what it means to endure.

Endurance, in Greek, is "*hupomonē*." It is a noun that refers to a state of constancy, a steadfastness; it is to endure patiently. The meaning of the root of the word implies hope. The *ESV Hebrew-Greek Word Study Bible* says that endurance is "a bearing up under."

**Read Hebrews 12:1-4.**

**How are we to run?** ____________________

**Have we experienced opposition or hardship to the extent of Jesus?** ______

We are to fix our eyes on Jesus and run with perseverance. We are strengthened when we consider what He endured so that we "don't become weary and lose heart."

**Read Hebrews 10:35-39.**

**What is needed to receive what God has promised?**

_______________________________________________

**According to verse 37, where are we to set our sights?**

_______________________________________________

**What is it the righteous are to live by?**

_______________________________________________

**We <u>do not</u> belong to (circle all that apply):**

**Those who endure and win**

**Those who shrink back**

**Those who finish victorious**

**Those who are destroyed**

Jesus kept His trust in God; kept His hope set on His reward; and kept His focus heavenward—three things needed to keep enduring.

Paul was comforted and encouraged by the Holy Spirit many times not to lose heart. He endured by God's all-sufficient power and grace. Through every trial, myriad difficulties and opposition, Paul kept the faith. He never gave up and never turned back. Encouragement can be found on his perseverance from his letters.

**Read Galatians 6:9.**

**Complete his instruction:**

**Don't become weary in ____________________ .**

**You will reap a harvest if you**

**____________________________________________ .**

**What does he tell us to do in 1 Corinthians 15:58?**

________________________________________________________

**Write-to-memorize 1 Corinthians 16:13:**

________________________________________________________

________________________________________________________

**"Here is a trustworthy saying" found in 2 Timothy 2:12. What is it?**

________________________________________________________

Finishing strong means not giving up and to keep on doing good. Let nothing move you, dear Christian. Stand firm and be ever on your guard. Hear your Heavenly Father telling you to just get up one more time than you fall.

Day 4

# Paul's Finish

So we are quickly learning that it is not how you began that really matters...but how you finish.

The fact that God makes us a new creation in Christ demonstrates that fact. And the continuing work of creating us in Christ to be His masterpiece proves it even further.

## Paul's Priorities

Just look at Paul. God prepared Paul for the same things for which we all are being prepared—to finish. Oh, and not *just* finish. But finish strong! To do that, we must firmly establish some high-ranking priorities.

"The purpose for which [Christ] took hold of Paul on the Damascus road and for which He takes hold of us individually is to bring us to faith in Himself. He died to save us not only from the guilt of sin but from sin's power and pollution. He died not to make us happy but to make us holy."

~*Jerry Bridges*
*The Practice of Godliness*

**Read Philippians 3:10-16.**

**What did Paul want to know?**

________________________________________

**Who should view things in such a way (vs 15)?**

________________________________________

**We are to "live up to" what we have already**

________________________________________.

Paul ran a disciplined and intensely motivated race. He strained to finish, not for selfish reasons, however. His desire was to finish the work God gave him to do, motivated by God's promised reward.

"One thing" speaks to priority. Paul emphasized that his "one thing" was to "strain ahead, "press on to win the prize."

**Read Acts 20:24.**

**What meant more to him than life itself?**

________________________________________

"My only aim" also speaks to priority. He had his life set on finishing the race by completing the task of "testifying to the good news of God's grace."

The prepared-to-finish of us all is living and sharing the gospel. It is the ultimate work prepared for us. The ultimate finish of us all is the finish of Paul, as stated in Acts 20:24.

**To what level is that a priority in your life?**

____________________________________________

Near the end of his life, Paul wrote to his "son in the faith."

**Read 2 Timothy 4:6-8.**

**What can you learn about when Paul wrote this letter from verse 6?**

____________________________________________

**According to verse 7, what could he look back and confidently say?**

____________________________________________

**How might that apply in your life?**

____________________________________________

**For what in your life right now do you need to keep the faith?** ______________________________________

**What awaited him (vs 8)?**

____________________________________________

**Is it awarded to him only?** __________________________

"The prize of this calling toward which [Paul] presses forward with all his might, is the everlasting, heavenly glory."
*~Jac J. Müller*

**What are we to long for?** ______________________________

We are prepared to do good works to finish and say, as Christ, when standing before God:

> **"I have brought You glory on earth by finishing the work You gave Me to do."**
> (Jn 17:4)

The glory of God and the glory of heaven as our focus and our goal make for strong motivation to finish.

And the efficacious grace of God demonstrated toward Paul—a grace **certain** to produce His intended results—is the same grace preparing us for a strong finish.

Day 5

## Prizes, Rewards, and Crowns—Oh My!

Yesterday we read of the "crown of righteousness" to which Paul looked forward—a crown promised by the Lord, not only to him but "all who long for His appearing" (2 Tm 4:8).

To keep us in the race, today we will consider more deeply the prize held out before us.

All that glitters is not gold, however.

**Look at Philippians 4:1 and 1 Thessalonians 2:19-20 to see the "crown" to which Paul referred.**

As an evangelist, Paul considered those he won to Christ his great reward. This crown was the fruit of a workman approved.

**Read 1 Peter 5:1-4.**

**This "crown of glory" is for whom?**

________________________________________

**Read James 1:12 in the sidebar.**

**Those that persevere under trial are called what?**

________________________________________

**What sort of crown do they receive for standing the test?**

________________________________________

**Who is it for?** ________________________________

Those who love the Lord and faithfully endure are awarded by the Lord the crown of life—a promise to keep you running strong!

"Blessed is the one who perseveres under trial because, having stood the test, that person will receive the crown of life that the Lord has promised to those who love Him."

(*Jms 1:12*)

## Prized Rewards Paul Kept Straining Toward

Paul had a real sense of the prize the Lord had waiting for him. It kept him going…and going strong.

**Read 2 Corinthians 5:1-5.**

**For what prize was he longing?**

______________________________________________

**Read 1 Corinthians 9:24-27.**

**How does Paul say we should run?**

______________________________________________

**Is it a race that requires training? If so, what kind?**

______________________________________________

**For what prize?** _________________________________

**What type of crown?** _____________________________

**From verse 26, we are not to run:**

______________________________________________

**How are we to run so as "not to be disqualified for the prize"?**

**Disciplined**

**Fast**

**Undisciplined**

**Slow**

Paul was resolutely convinced of the Lord's promise of resurrection and eternal life. His aim was his heavenly home. And he ran in such a disciplined way to be sure it was a prize he would not forfeit.

**How does heaven's glory propel your finish?**

______________________________________________

______________________________________________

**Are you "straining toward" the prize?**

______________________________________________

**There is a dire warning given by our Lord. Find out what it is from Matthew 6:2:**

______________________________________________

**What does hold promise for the life to come, according to 2 Timothy 4:8?**

______________________________________________

"For the Son of Man is going to come in His Father's glory with His angels, and then He will reward each person according to what they have done." (*Mt 16:27*)

Finishing strong is to meet God face-to-face on the other side of this life and say we ***are*** the work He prepared...and have done the work He prepared for us to do for His glory and praise.

Until that great and glorious day, can we live prepared to say, as Paul:

**Prepared to Say**

"I consider my life worth nothing to me; my only aim is to finish the race and complete the task the Lord Jesus has given me—the task of testifying to the good news of God's grace" (Acts 20:24).

*WEEK TWELVE SUMMARY*

# Putting It Together

**DAY 1**

## Ephesians 2:10 Revisited

I spent months preparing.

I studied, researched, and carefully wrote. I became familiar with the topics, memorized the verses, and rehearsed the content. I prayed. And prayed.

The day came at last and finally I stood before the group to speak. At the first flutter of nerves, God reminded me that I was ready.

Prepared.

It's a state of being.

It comes when as a child of God, you know the Father is with you. It comes with the realization that His sovereign, sufficient Hand is at work in your life. And from such a faith, confidence flows.

When you can reflect upon a season or set of circumstances and come to the peaceful conclusion that God used it to prepare you, you are blessed, indeed!

And that's what Ephesians 2:10 is—a confidence booster. A faith-builder. A praise unto God.

### Putting the pieces of 2:10 together

The purpose of this study is for the reader to be able to say, "I am a masterpiece prepared. Prepared by God for good works, to reflect His glory."

So, here at Week 12, we'll assemble all the pieces and have a summary review so that you can say it, too.

We have discovered together that Ephesians 2:10 has two halves:

- o What God prepares
- o What God has prepared

The first half is what God prepares *in us* (through agents, experiences, trials and others).

The second half is what God has prepared *for us* (by giving, serving, mentoring, etc.).

We further considered the verse in this way: We are the workmanship God is creating through Christ Jesus so that we may do a work He has planned for us to do. It could look like this:

**by God**

**We are a prepared work to do a work prepared**

**by God**

**Review Ephesians 2:1-10 (nice and slow).**

Ephesians 2 opens with how we **once** walked and builds to 2:10 in how we **now** walk—as His workmanship doing His will.

**Write 2 Corinthians 5:17.**

________________________________________________

________________________________________________

**We are a new creation! It is important to make the distinction made in Ephesians 2:10:**

**We are created in** ________________________________

The path God prepared Paul to travel and the works God did through him along that path were used in perfecting Paul, the masterpiece of God.

**From Ephesians 2, note what we are in Christ.**

**Vs 5:** ______________________________

**Vs 6:** ______________________________

**Vs 8:** ______________________________

**Vs 10:** ______________________________

**Though once dead (vs 1), we are now alive (vs 5) because of (vs 4):**

**1)** ______________________________

**2)** ______________________________

What is all this preparing for? For what purpose is God creating us into His workmanship? The answer is also found in Ephesians 2:10. The hina clause swings the reason to purpose.

**God is doing all that creating so that:**

______________________________

He is masterfully working us to do good works…to walk in them in an honorable, God-glorifying way.

The man who penned this specific verse, under the direction of the Holy Spirit, is proof of its validity. He is living example of the truth of Ephesians 2:10, a fact to which he testified in many of his epistles.

**Read Ephesians 3:7.**

**How did Paul become a servant of the gospel?**

______________________________

______________________________

The grace of God that saved and the power of God that transformed Saul to become the Apostle Paul is the same preparing you, my friend.

Day 2

# Masterful Masterpiece

This second day of our summary review, we'll revisit *masterpiece.*

"Masterpiece" in Greek is *poiēma* (poy'–ay–mah).

Here is a poem I wrote to summarize Ephesians 2; but, really, it's a poem about a *poiēma*...a poem about the masterpiece of you.

*Poiēma*—
Created by the Father's Hand.
*Poiēma*—
To dwell in a heavenly land.
*Poiēma*—
It's all a matter of God's grace.
*Poiēma*—
In Christ Jesus, it comes by faith.
*Poiēma*—
I once was dead and now alive;
*Poiēma*—
A masterpiece, prepared to thrive.
*Poiēma*—
He writes His story across my heart.
*Poiēma*—
A poem to praise His glory;
how great Thou art!

## Wrapping up the Masterpiece

Say it: *Masterpiece.*

It suits you.

Really, it does!

The beauty of it is that you don't have to be a completed masterpiece to be one. We are all a work in progress. We are fashioned by the cross of Christ and our God of integrity will finish what He has promised. He won't lay down His shaping tools until our earthly days are done.

But what does it mean for us to live as a masterpiece?

"The renewal of the new self is in knowledge. It takes place as a believer comes to a personal, deep knowledge of and fellowship with Christ. And the renewal is in the image of its Creator; its goal is to make believers like Him, for the new self was created to be like God. Adam was created in the image of God…though this image was not erased (but only effaced) by the Fall, yet it was corrupted and needs to be repaired and renewed. Christians become increasingly like the Lord as they refresh their new natures, yielding to the Holy Spirit's sanctifying work. And in the resurrection… the task of restoring God's image will be complete, for 'we shall be like Him' (1 Jn 3:2)."

~*The Bible Knowledge Commentary New Testament* (*Geisler*)

**Read Colossians 3:10.**

**The new self is being** ____________________

**in** ______________________________

**and in** ___________________________

What kind of masterpiece? One like Him—The Master! But that takes renewing.

Remember, He is Creator. As a human cannot fully develop without relationship, we cannot become His masterpiece without a relationship with Christ. We must abide in Him, placing our lives in His hands for shaping and molding.

**What have you tried by your own might?**

____________________________________________

Though he endured such hardship, Paul told the Corinthians with fervor that, though he was wasting away on the outside, he was being renewed day-by-day on the inside (2 Cor 4:16).

We can learn from Paul's letter to the Ephesians about living as this new creation.

**Read Ephesians 4:17-5:2.**

**According to verse 23, we are made new in the**

____________________________________________.

**Verse 22 states we are to "put off our old self." Verse 24 states we are to do what with our new self?**

Masterpiece: it's not something *you* make, or something *you* create, it's something you become—by the Master's Hand.

________________________________________

**Whom are we created to be like (vs 24)?**

________________________________________

**From verses 25-32, check the correct response to the action:**

| TO DO | NOT TO DO | |
|---|---|---|
| ☐ | ☐ | **Put off falsehood (v25)** |
| ☐ | ☐ | **Harbor anger (vs 26)** |
| ☐ | ☐ | **Give the devil a foothold (vs 27)** |
| ☐ | ☐ | **Work in order to share (vs 28)** |
| ☐ | ☐ | **Say whatever you want (vs 29)** |
| ☐ | ☐ | **Grieve the Holy Spirit (vs 30)** |
| ☐ | ☐ | **Forgive (vs 32)** |

**Ephesians 5:1 tells us to be**

________________________________________

**We are to live a life of ________________________.**

Living a life of love is to live as His masterpiece—for that is to live like the Master. Oh, and it's not just a piece of the Master...but full of the Master.

Living a life of love is to be a Master-full Masterpiece.

# Prepositional Preparedness

He had a God-sized job to do…but he was hardly ready.

So the Lord blinded him by dazzling glory, and he was never the same.

Saul, the Pharisee from Tarsus, was prepared **by** other Christians (namely, Ananias and Barnabas). He was prepared **by** the Holy Spirit, **by** faith, prayer, and the Word. He was prepared **to** listen, **to** move on, and **to** grow—**to** become Paul, the servant-apostle of God.

**In** seclusion, suffering, battles, and even **in** weakness, he was further prepared **for** missions and ministry works. He was also prepared **for** mentoring and, ultimately, **for** death.

Mostly, Paul was prepared **to** hope and **to** reflect the Lord's glory.

All the same prepositions God uses to prepare you. I guess you can call it prepositional preparedness.

## Preparing Prepositions: By / For / To / In

And just as God used all things in Paul's life, He can take all things in yours to work them all together for your good, too (Rm 8:28).

**Because we are all being**

________________________________________

________________________________________

**(Complete the thought from the second half of 2 Corinthians 3:18 above).**

Once in Christ, we are ever-increasingly being transformed into His image.

Check what was used by God to prepare Paul:

- ☐ **Education** (under Gamaliel)
- ☐ **Training** (in the Law)
- ☐ **Trade** (as tentmaker)
- ☐ **Position** (as Pharisee)
- ☐ **Citizenship** (as a Roman)
- ☐ **Language** (to speak Aramaic)
- ☐ **Suffering** (his "thorn in the flesh")

**What would *your* list look like?**

_______________________________________________

_______________________________________________

_______________________________________________

Yes! The Holy Son of God prepares us— <u>from</u> Fallen . . . <u>for</u> Eternity.

**Read Acts 26:22.**

**Paul had help that comes from ______________________.**

**Match the type of help Paul had (from the Word Bank) to the Verse.**

| | |
|---|---|
| **A) Strengthened** | ☐ **Acts 16:9** |
| **B) Warning** | ☐ **Acts 18:9-10** |
| **C) Encouragement** | ☐ **Acts 22:17** |
| **D) Direction** | ☐ **Acts 27:22** |
| **E) Assurance** | ☐ **2 Tm 4:16-17** |

At every turn, God was there to help Paul and further prepare him for the next thing. And when things got difficult, God provided much needed comfort.

**Match the Lord's comfort in each situation with its verse.**

| | |
|---|---|
| **Acts 23:11** | **In the face of suffering** |
| **1 Tm 1:12** | **In the face of fear** |
| **2 Tm 4:18** | **In the face of death** |

God is in the business of preparing saints so that we who hope in Christ "might be to the praise of His glory" (Eph 1:12).

Yes! The Holy Son of God prepares us—**from** Fallen and **for** Eternity.

## Day 4
# First Things First

It's important to get the right order of things—to get first things first. (Especially with grace and works!)

Paul carefully established there was first A then B—first grace then works. We are saved by grace—that's A, the first thing.Then, by faith and the continued working of grace, we are to work—that's B.

First A then B.

We can't neglect either—grace or works.

First A. But always B.

We can't neglect B, either.

Works are not a means of salvation, by any means; but the fruit of it. I once heard it said that works are not the cause of our salvation, but its consequence.

"Therefore, my beloved brothers, be steadfast, immovable, always abounding in the work of the Lord, knowing that in the Lord your labor is not in vain."

(*1 Corinthians 15:58, ESV*)

## First A Then B

God first does His good work in us so that we can do a good work.

This is no more evident than in the life of Paul. God prepared Paul to do the work God had prepared for him to do.

**From Romans 1:1 below:**

**Circle the ministry positions God had for Paul.**

**Underline the ministry positions God has for us all.**

**"Paul, a servant of Christ Jesus, called to be an apostle and set apart for the gospel of God."**

**Read Ephesians 3:7-11.**

**According to Ephesians 3:7, how did he become a servant?**

**The Roman Governor**

**God's grace**

**The High Priest**

**The working of God's power**

**He received God's grace for what purpose (vs 8)?**

______________________________________________

**What is now for the church to do (vs 10)?**

______________________________________________

**Look up 1 Corinthians 4:1 to learn how Paul wanted to be regarded.** ______________________________

**Read 2 Corinthians 6:4-10 to see to what extent he was willing to be God's servant.**

God's prepared work for Paul was as preacher to the Gentiles. He spent 20 years traveling to plant churches throughout Asia. But, foremost, he always considered himself to be a servant...a servant of the Lord.

**As stated in Matthew 12:17, Jesus fulfilled the prophecy of Isaiah. To what is He referred as in Matthew 12:18?**

________________________________________

**How does Peter say we are to live in 1 Peter 2:16?**

________________________________________

Noble works are those that serve God and others. So, if you're not sure how to work, serve.

**Write 1 Peter 4:10.**

________________________________________

________________________________________

God made ready works for us to do—that we should live holy lives as we walk in the works He prepared for us.

Work as one who serves—it's the first thing.

"If anyone serves, they should do so with the strength God provides, so that in all things God may be praised through Jesus Christ. To Him be the glory and the power for ever and ever. Amen."

(*1 Peter 4:11*)

## Day 5
# Finishing Prepared

My son ran cross country in high school. I'll never forget his first race. We rose in what seemed like the middle of night to journey quite a distance to the venue. We arrived in the dark, but the temperatures were already high. The runners readied in the breaking of dawn; and, as the sun came up over the dew-covered field, the humidity rose with the sun.

I chose a spot several yards down the course. I wasn't concerned with the starting line or how he got out of the gate. I wanted to see how he was running the race. I watched and watched for him. I hoped and prayed his training and his coach made him ready. As he passed, I took an assessment and cheered him on. I then moved to another point across the field, to wait once again for him to pass. I did that several times. I longed to lend encouragement and to check both his gaze and his gait.

I didn't care if he won. And I wasn't concerned with his time. I just wanted him to run. He was challenged by the battling factors of heat, fatigue, and endurance. So, more than anything, I wanted him to finish. In doing so, I wanted him to gain the assurance that God was with him to help him through and to gain confidence that, together, they could.

At last I moved toward the finish. I shouldered my way through to the sideline, short of the finish line. When he came into view, I paced alongside and cheered him across the finish—meeting him with a cool cup of water and a hearty "Well done!"

**Make it a habit to check often your gaze and your gait by asking these questions:**

**Is my gaze focused on the eternal and the will of God?**

**Is my gait faithful and consistent, striding on the right path?**

## Racing Challenges

As the heat posed great challenge for him, temptations are the great foe of the Christian runner.

**What is our Lord's warning in Matthew 26:41?**

______________________________________________

**We will encounter daily temptations that try to throw us off course and out of the race. What should we be careful not to say, as found in James 1:13?**

______________________________________________

**Because Jesus suffered when He was tempted, is He able to help us? (Find the answer in Hebrews 2:18.)**

______________________________________________

**We are told that we will suffer. Read James 1:2-8. What will the testing of our faith produce?**

______________________________________________

**What will we be for allowing perseverance to finish its work (vs 4)?** ______________________________

**Read James 1:12-15.**

**The blessed who persevere under trial are promised to receive** ______________________________.

"So do not throw away your confidence; it will be richly rewarded. You need to persevere so that when you have done the will of God, you will receive what He has promised. For, 'In just a little while, He who is coming will come and will not delay."

(*Hebrews 10:35-37*)

**What is the danger when we give in to temptation?**

_______________________________________________

James helps prepare our faith by providing practical application in suffering, trials, and temptation.

**And he cheers the runner on with this encouragement found in James 5:7-8:**

_______________________________________________

_______________________________________________

"I am coming soon. Hold on to what you have, so that no one will take your crown."

"Look, I am coming soon! My reward is with Me, and I will give to each person according to what they have done."

*~Jesus (Rev 3:11; 22:12)*

Amos, the prophet, told the people to "prepare to meet your God." That is the finish line of our faith. And therein lies great promise, for there He is preparing for our finish.

**Read John 14:2-3.**

**Who else is also preparing?**

_______________________________________________

**What is He preparing?**

_______________________________________________

We read elsewhere in the New Testament that God is preparing an eternal dwelling for His people (Heb. 11:16). He is preparing a new heaven and a new earth "prepared as a bride beautifully dressed for her husband" (Rev 21:1-2).

Keep running the race…finish, prepared. His great reward awaits you.

**Read Matthew 25:31-36.**

**"Then the King will say to those on His right:**
**'Come, you who are blessed by My Father;**

_______________________________________________

_______________________________________________

A kingdom awaits...one prepared since Creation.

You, dear saint, *are* the Prepared—just like you are the redeemed, saved, loved, adopted child of God.

Live the life of the prepared...*all the way home.*

> With this in mind, I pray that our God will make you worthy of His calling, and that by His power He will bring to fruition your every desire for goodness and your every deed prompted by faith. I pray this so that the name of our Lord Jesus may be glorified in you, and you in Him, according to the grace of our God and the Lord Jesus Christ
>
> (2 Thessalonians 1:11-12 adapted).

Live prepared—for He **has** made you ready.

Ready enough to say of yourself:

**Prepared to Say**

I am "His masterpiece, created in Christ Jesus for good works, which God prepared beforehand, that [ I ] should walk in them (Eph 2:10).

## Works Cited


- (n.d.). Retrieved from *www.miliatryfieldmanuals.net*
- (n.d.). Retrieved from *www.naval-military-press.com*
- (n.d.). Retrieved from Dictionary.com: *http://dictionary.reference.com/browse/prepared?s=t*
- (n.d.). Retrieved from Free Dictionary: *http://www.thefreedictionary.com/turning+point*
- (n.d.). Retrieved from Bible Hub: *http://biblehub.com/greek/2677.htm*
- Bible Gateway Study Tools, Encyclopedia of the Bible. (n.d.).
- *Bible Hub.* (n.d.). Retrieved from *http://biblehub.com/hebrew/4908.htm*
- *Bible Hub.* (n.d.). Retrieved from *http://biblehub.com/greek/2677.htm*
- *Bible Hub/HELP Word Studies.* (n.d.). Retrieved from *http://biblehub.com/greek/3339.htm*
- Borchert, G. L. (n.d.). Perseverance. *In Holman Illustrated Bible Dictionary.*
- Brewer, B. (n.d.). Good Mentoring. *Christianity Today.*
- Bridges, J. (n.d.). *Pursuit of Holiness.*
- Bridges, J. (n.d.). *The Practice of Godliness.*
- Chambers, O. (n.d.). *In The Westminster Collection of Christian Quotes.Encyclopedia of the Bible/ Humility.* (n.d.). Retrieved from BibleGateway Study
- Tools: *https://www.biblegateway.com/resources/encyclopedia-ofthe-bible/Humility*
- Geisler, N. L. (n.d.). Colossians. *In The Bible Knowledge Commentary New Testament* (p. 681).
- *Hebrew-Greek Key Word Study Bible.* (n.d.).
- Hillis, D. (n.d.). DayBook of Promise.
- Hoehner. (n.d.). The Bible Knowledge Commentary Old Testament.
- Lucado, M. (n.d.). *You'll Get Through This.*
- Lucado, M. (n.d.). *It's Not About Me.*
- McCasland, D. (n.d.). *The Quotable Oswald Chambers.*
- Meyer, F. B. (n.d.). *15 Key Studies from the Heart of Ephesians: A Topical Commentary.*
- Nouwen, H. (n.d.). *Turn My Mourning Into Dancing.*
- Packer, J. I. (n.d.). *Knowing Christianity.*
- Shelly, R. (n.d.). *Going on to Maturity.*
- Stott, J. (n.d.). *The Radical Disciple.*
- Strong, T. (n.d.). Parable. *In Holman Illustratied Bible Dictionary* (p. 1244).
- Strong's Concordance. (n.d.).
- Swindoll, C. (n.d.). *Paul: A Man of Grace and Grit.*
- Thayers Greek Lexicon
- The Bible Knowledge Commentary New Testament. (n.d.).
- The Bible Knowledge Commentary New Testament. (n.d.). In *Ephesians.*
- Walker, W. L. (n.d.). In *Standard Bible Encyclopedia.*